PLAY LIKE
LIVERPOOL FC

Cover design: Rick Cooke, Glen Hind
Proofing: William Hughes and Alan Jewell

Produced by Sport Media, Trinity Mirror North West

Executive Editor: Ken Rogers. Senior Editor: Steve Hanrahan
Senior Production Editor: Paul Dove. Senior Art Editor: Rick Cooke
Sub Editors: Roy Gilfoyle, James Cleary, Michael Haydock, Adam Oldfield
Designers: Glen Hind, Colin Sumpter, Barry Parker, Lee Ashun,
Alison Gilliland, Jamie Dunmore, James Kenyon, Lisa Critchley
Writers: Chris McLoughlin, David Randles,
Gavin Kirk, John Hynes, Simon Hughes, William Hughes, Alan Jewell
Sales and Marketing Manager: Elizabeth Morgan
Sales and marketing assistant: Karen Cadman

Published in Great Britain in 2009 by: Trinity Mirror Sport Media,
PO Box 48, Old Hall Street, Liverpool L69 3EB.
All Rights Reserved. No part of this publication may be reproduced, stored in a retrieval system, or transmitted in any form, or by any means, electronic, mechanical, photocopying, recording or otherwise without the prior permission in writing of the copyright holders, nor be otherwise circulated in any form of binding or cover other than in which it is published and without a similar condition being imposed on the subsequent publisher.

ISBN: 9781906802134

Photographs: John Cocks, John Powell, Andrew Powell, Trinity Mirror, Mirrorpix, PA Photos

Printed by Korotan

RAFAEL BENITEZ

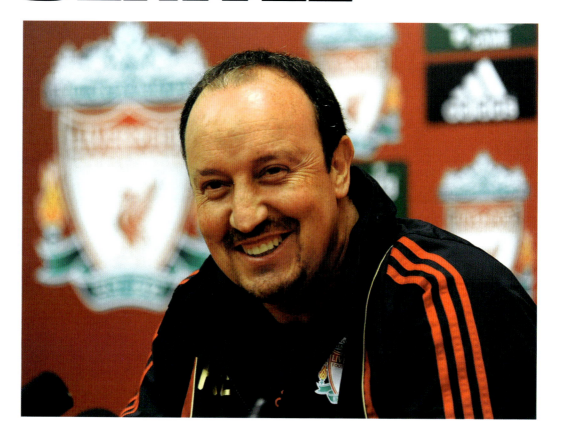

I hope this book gives you an insight into what it is like to play for Liverpool and what you must do to try and play like Liverpool yourself

Welcome to Play Like Liverpool. For me, if a player wants to play for Liverpool then he must work hard, have quality, a good mentality and train well.

Training is very important. It is the only way to improve. Training regularly is the only way to make it as a professional player.

If you are good enough you can maybe play some games for a big club but if you want to stay and have a good career there you have to train well and be professional.

The main thing is to keep the passion and the belief while continuing to work hard. Together with the right mentality, a player must also have confidence in themselves.

I hope this book gives you an insight into what it is like to play for Liverpool and what you must do to try and play like Liverpool yourself.

Rafa Benitez

STEVEN GERRARD

It doesn't matter how much talent or ability you're born with. If you don't work hard then you won't get to where you want to be

I used to play football all the time on the streets in Huyton and get kicked from pillar to post by the older boys. That sort of education for a footballer is priceless. It certainly toughened me up and I think those lessons have helped me throughout my career.

It doesn't matter how much talent or ability you're born with, if you don't work hard on improving then you won't get to where you want to be. No-one is born with the perfect technique, you learn and improve all the time as you go along and it's one of those things that gets better the more you practice.

If you want to Play Like Liverpool you've also got to think like a Liverpool player and that means being dedicated to improving. You get out of football what you put into it. Give it your best shot and who knows where it can lead?

FERNANDO TORRES

I hope that by passing some of my tips on that maybe I can help some of you one day play for our club

I see a lot of kids in Liverpool playing football. I was always playing when I was a kid too, hitting the ball against a wall or with my friends and my brother.

It is important to practice. In fact, it's not even practising. If you enjoy football, you will play as much as you can and then you will get better.

I also hope you enjoy this book. I appreciate all the support I have been given by Liverpool fans since I came to the club and I hope that by passing some of my tips on that maybe I can help some of you one day play for our club.

For me, striker is the best position on the pitch but whichever position you play in there will be something in this book to help you improve your game.

Good luck.

JAMIE CARRAGHER

In this book I talk about the attributes you need to play at centre-back. I hope it helps and you enjoy it. and enjoy your football

When I was growing up I played as much football with my mates as I could and I still play footy now with my own kids in the garden.

I was a striker when I was a kid and now, I think some people find that hard to believe because I play centre-back. It's not the most glamorous position on the pitch but it is an important role.

In this book I talk about the attributes you need to play at centre-back such as anticipation, positioning, tackling and good communication but if you don't put the graft in, eat well or you lose sight of the basics then you'll get nowhere.

Enjoy the book and enjoy your football.

CONTENTS

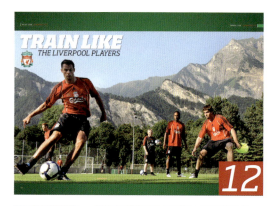 12

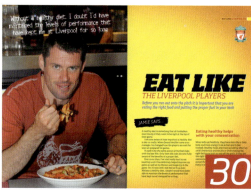 30

 78

 98

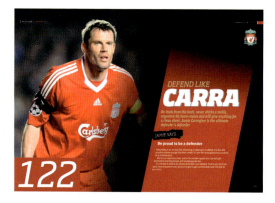 122

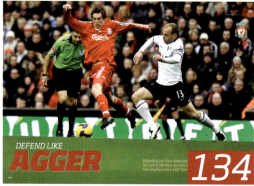 134

 158

 168

KEEP FIT LIKE THE REDS — 42

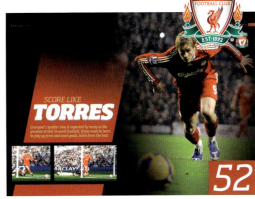

SCORE LIKE TORRES — 52

STOP THE OPPOSITION LIKE MASCHERANO — 106

WORK LIKE DIRK — 114

ATTACK FROM THE BACK LIKE JOHNSON — 146

KEEP GOAL LIKE PEPE — 148

PLAY LIKE THE LEGENDS — 178

CELEBRATE LIKE THE PLAYERS — 198

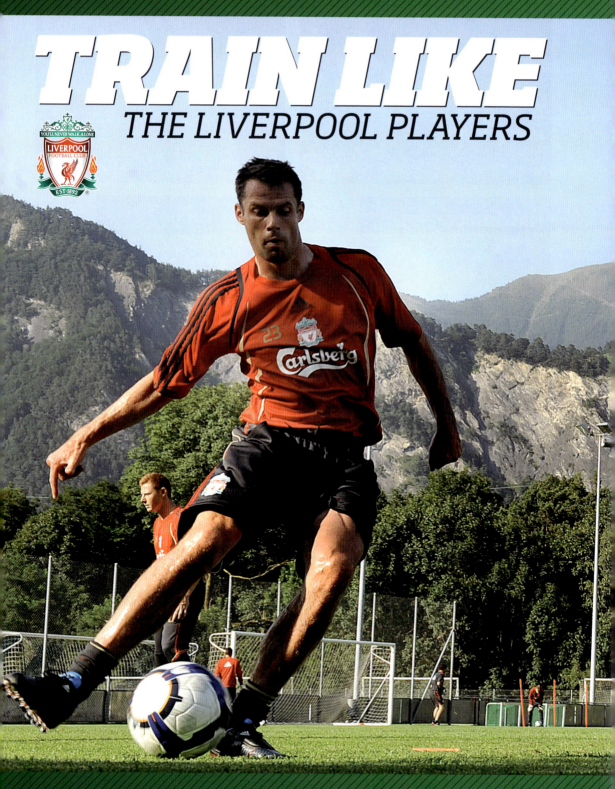

PLAY LIKE LIVERPOOL FC

TRAIN LIKE
THE LIVERPOOL PLAYERS

TRAIN LIKE LIVERPOOL FC

PLAY LIKE LIVERPOOL FC

Warming up for the action

Stretching the muscles before exercising or playing is essential for the Liverpool players, however youngsters' bodies are more flexible than teenagers and adults and this doesn't need to be overdone

STRETCH TIP...

QUADS: Stretching with a friend or teammate can help you balance like Steven and Dirk in these pictures. Here they are pulling their legs back to stretch their quadriceps. The 'quads' are four muscles on the front of the thigh and are the strongest muscles in the human body.

If you don't feel a stretch in the front of your thigh, pull your foot further back and push your foot down into your palm.

TRAIN LIKE LIVERPOOL FC

STRETCH TIP...

CALVES: Place your hands on your teammates' shoulders.
Step back with your right leg, keeping it straight, while the left knee bends. With both heels on the floor, lean forward by bending your left knee until you feel a stretch in your calf. Hold. Repeat on the other side.

| PLAY LIKE LIVERPOOL FC

STRETCH TIP...

HAMSTRINGS: Place right leg straight out in front of you while the left knee stays on the floor. Keep the right knee straight during the stretch. Keep the arch in your back as you reach to touch your toes, and pull them towards you. Repeat with the other side.

Pull your toes back to feel your hamstring stretch

STRETCH TIP...

GROIN: Steven demonstrates how you can stretch your groin and hamsting at the same time by kicking your leg high in the air and pressing down on your knee. Try clapping underneath like Jamie and Fernando as you move forward and alternate.

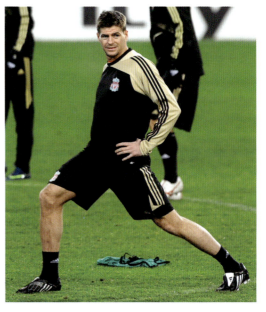

TRAIN LIKE LIVERPOOL FC

PLAY LIKE LIVERPOOL FC

Keeping an eye on the players: Mauricio Pellegrino

Work hard in training and that hard work will pay off on the pitch. Rafa's first team coach tells us how the Reds do it

MAURICIO SAYS...

My job consists of working with Paco De Miguel, Sammy Lee and Xavi Valero (Goalkeeping Coach) to organise the training sessions for the week ahead.

Technical analyst Dave McDonough and Doctor Waller are also involved in the process.

Every morning we decide on the training cycle depending on how many games we have that week. First there is a meeting to discuss the number of players available. The doctor will tell us who can or can't take part.

Depending on injuries you can sometimes have 15 players, sometimes 22, plus goalkeepers.

It's vital to establish just how many of those are available in order to plan the sessions.

Within that we also have to cater for the needs of different individuals.

After the initial chat we establish the objective of the day and dynamic of the session.

Some of it will be with me, another part with Sammy, another with Pako and another with Rafa.

The routine is always organised with the next game in mind. We'll have watched videos of our opponents so we can work on set pieces with their strengths and weaknesses.

When the session is finalised we show it to Rafa Benitez and sometimes he might want to change something if he feels it's necessary.

TRAIN LIKE LIVERPOOL FC

STRENGTH TIP...

It's important that you don't get knocked off the ball too easily. Try using your shoulders to lean into your opponent and protect the ball.

Weekly training schedule

This obviously varies depending on how many games we have during the week.

When you have two or three fixtures you are unable to do a lot of physical work.

Rest and proper recovery are vital when you play a league match at the weekend then Champions League, then another match at the weekend.

If it's just one game in seven days we train in different ways because the players are obviously fresher.

We can do more muscular work that allows them to build strength and endurance.

Training on the day before a game

Obviously you don't want the players to do too much because that won't help them when the game arrives.

Instead we focus on getting them ready for the next day by doing stretching and preparing properly. Also we will do lots of work on tactics as that way it is fresh in the minds.

PLAY LIKE LIVERPOOL FC

Training on the day of a game

The physical objective is to increase the temperature of the body. Paco does that in a gradual manner.

It starts in the changing room with stretching and mobility exercises.

Then out on the pitch Sammy takes over with some more mobility work. If you watch the pre-match routines you will notice the majority of those exercises are done with the ball.

That creates good habits and gets the players' line of passing correct.

TRAIN LIKE LIVERPOOL FC

Shooting exercise

The players will play a one-two with the coach on the edge of the area before shooting at goal. It's done at pace and helps the players ready themselves for the 90 minutes ahead.

Also, as it involves scoring goals, it puts the players in a positive frame of mind just before kick-off.

Keeping the ball

We do a variety of possession drills involving one, two, three and four touches.

This obviously gives the players a feel for the ball and (when four touches are allowed) lets them run with it.

When we want to work on just passing we cut down the space and touches.

Obviously it's very hard to take three or four touches in a 30m rectangle. Therefore they have to pass it if they want to retain the ball for their team.

Often we use two teams of four players with two jokers. A joker is someone who is always with the team in possession.

When the ball switches sides these players do the same. It's usually some of the midfielders who fill this role because they are obviously key players when it comes to keeping possession in a game.

POSSESSION TIP...

IMPROVE YOUR TOUCH: Keeping the ball in a small area is a great way of improving your touch and passing in tight situations. A group of players form a circle and one player starts in the middle, like Emiliano Insua in this picture. The players on the outside have to control the ball with one touch and pass it quickly to a teammate before the man in the middle intercepts it. If he does manage to block it, it's your turn to go in the middle and try to win the ball back. You can also speed the game up by making it one touch only and this will force you to think quickly and make a swift pass.

PLAY LIKE LIVERPOOL FC

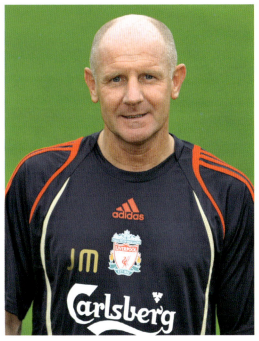

Reserves coach John McMahon believes a simple way to improve your game is to get outside in the fresh air with a ball at your feet as often as possible

Find a wall and just knock the ball back and forward; right foot, left foot, bump, bump, bump

PRACTICE TIP...

BALL TO WALL: Kick the ball against the wall and aniticipate where it is going to go. Control it and then hit it back with your other foot. Vary how close you stand to the wall. Get close up and try quick one touch passes to the wall, without needing to control it. Stand further back and pick targets on the wall to practice your accuracy.

JOHN SAYS...

Get out there and play

Kids need to be working all the time on touch and passing.

I'm from the old school where growing up we never had the distractions of computers and computer games.

I was always outside with my ball with my mates or even just by myself.

That's one of the simplest messages I could give any kid growing up who wants to improve his game.

Leave the computer games and get outside in the fresh air with your ball.

The only way you become a better player is by having more touches and more time on the ball.

TRAIN LIKE LIVERPOOL FC

Liverpool legend Kevin Keegan uses the wall at the Melwood training ground back in the '70s

Practice using both feet as often as you can

Just keep using your left foot and right foot all the time. Develop both of them.

Find a wall and just knock the ball back and forward; right foot, left foot, bump, bump, bump.

It doesn't matter whether there's two of you or you are on your own, you can still focus on technique.

It's one of the first things Liverpool will look at in a player at whatever age.

Does he have the fundamentals? For me, the most basic fundamental is a player who can use both feet.

In many ways, playing with a wall's much better than playing with a mate if you're working

A ball's your best friend

on touch and things like that.

You get more touches of the ball with a wall and it comes straight back to you as hard as you hit it at the wall. The wall won't make mistakes getting the ball back to you, if it's not coming back to you then its your own error and you're constantly working to correct them.

You don't need money or fancy equipment to get better. A ball's your best friend.

PLAY LIKE LIVERPOOL FC

Discover the lost art of heading

It's something that I think has gone out of the game with kids a little bit. I don't see great heading of the ball in the youngsters playing in the streets.

You see kids ducking out the way of headers or trying to wait for the ball to drop for them. Be brave, keep your eyes open and get your forehead planted on the ball.

We used to play 60-second games and you can only score with your head.

It's a great skill to develop. In tight matches one header from a set-piece can mean the difference between winning and losing. It might be an attacking header that hits the net or a defensive header that clears a dangerous situation.

It's a hard thing, your head, so learn to use it well.

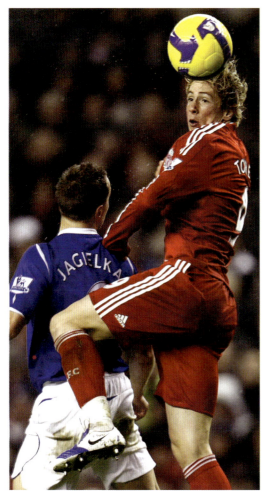

TRAIN LIKE LIVERPOOL FC

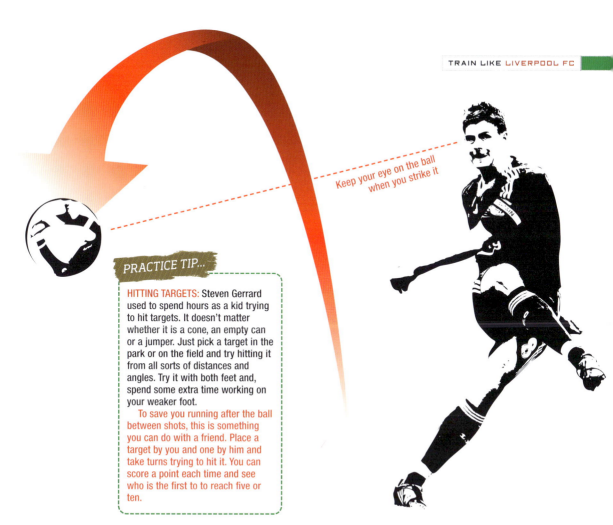

Keep your eye on the ball when you strike it

PRACTICE TIP...

HITTING TARGETS: Steven Gerrard used to spend hours as a kid trying to hit targets. It doesn't matter whether it is a cone, an empty can or a jumper. Just pick a target in the park or on the field and try hitting it from all sorts of distances and angles. Try it with both feet and, spend some extra time working on your weaker foot.

To save you running after the ball between shots, this is something you can do with a friend. Place a target by you and one by him and take turns trying to hit it. You can score a point each time and see who is the first to to reach five or ten.

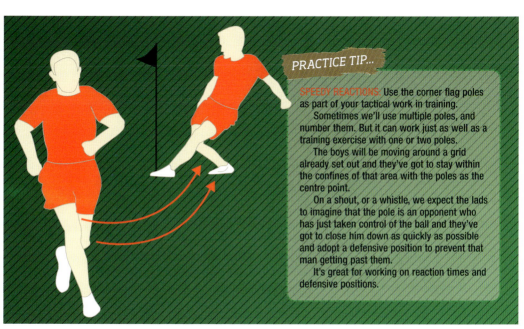

PRACTICE TIP...

SPEEDY REACTIONS: Use the corner flag poles as part of your tactical work in training.

Sometimes we'll use multiple poles, and number them. But it can work just as well as a training exercise with one or two poles.

The boys will be moving around a grid already set out and they've got to stay within the confines of that area with the poles as the centre point.

On a shout, or a whistle, we expect the lads to imagine that the pole is an opponent who has just taken control of the ball and they've got to close him down as quickly as possible and adopt a defensive position to prevent that man getting past them.

It's great for working on reaction times and defensive positions.

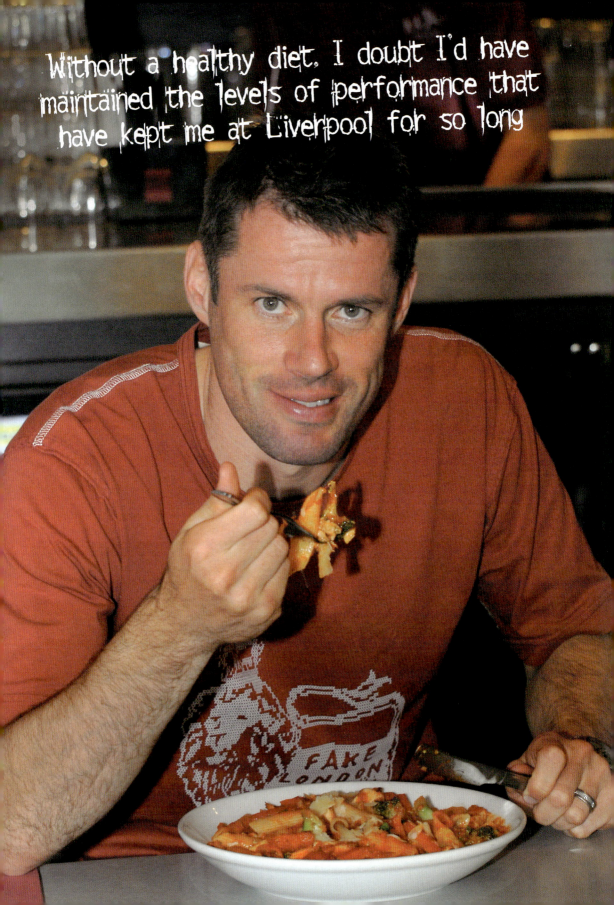

Without a healthy diet, I doubt I'd have maintained the levels of performance that have kept me at Liverpool for so long

EAT LIKE
THE LIVERPOOL PLAYERS

Before you run out on to the pitch it is important that you are eating the right food and putting the proper fuel in your tank

A healthy diet is something that all footballers must live by if they want to be right at the top of their game.

I became aware of how important a healthy diet is late on really. When Gerard Houllier came in as manager, he changed how the players ate and the way we prepared for games.

It used to be the same across all football clubs until the late 90s. Only then did clubs become fully aware of the benefits of a proper diet.

Ever since then, I've tried really hard to eat healthily and it has definitely helped improve my game as well as my fitness and longevity in the game. I'm 31 now and I still feel as fit as ever. Without a healthy diet, I doubt I would have been able to maintain the levels of performance that have kept me at Liverpool for so long.

Eating healthily helps with your concentration

When kids eat healthily, they have more life in their body and more energy to do active sports like football. Healthy foods also have a positive effect on a kid's behaviour and results in them making the right decisions both on and off the pitch. If they eat the right foods, they should have enough energy to concentrate and work hard for six or seven hours at school then have enough left in the tank for playing footy in the evenings too.

Jamie at his own restaurant, "Cafe Sports England" on Stanley Street in Liverpool

What I used to eat when I was a kid

When I was younger I knew what was good and bad for me. I grew up in a normal family where my dinner was cooked for me every night. My mum was quite conscious of eating healthily and there wasn't much chocolate or fizzy drinks in our cupboards. I always ate a lot of fruit instead.

But there's a lot more detail that goes into diet now. I understood that a regular trip to the fish and chip shop wasn't a good idea and that I shouldn't eat too many pizzas and burgers, but that was about it.

Now I know what to eat, rather than just what not to eat. When I started, I wasn't aware that pasta and chicken was good for you before training but not for your dinner. Also, it's not just black and white about what you eat, but when you eat as well.

I'm lucky that I've been educated on it at the club by dieticians that come to Melwood. So I try and make my kids eat the right things too. I'm fortunate enough that the job I've got allows me to provide a healthy alternative for my kids because it's not always cheap to eat healthily if you don't really know what you're doing.

What I eat now

I'm getting a bit older now, so I'm trying to vary my food to give me that bit more energy. Now, I eat some muesli, Alpen or porridge for breakfast rather than Shredded Wheat, which is what I used to have. Sometimes I will have some fruit salad or some boiled egg on toast for a bit of protein.

On a normal day, I'll have pasta and chicken then for evening I will eat grilled chicken or fish with some veg.

I'll have lots of fluids throughout the day as well, with water, apple juice or a smoothie.

Some people think footballers can stretch the boundaries a little bit more when the season ends and we go on holiday, but I don't think that's true. If anything, you can get away with having a few more treats during the course of the season because you're doing regular exercise then and find it easier to burn the fat off quickly. In the summer, when we get a chance to relax, the body slows down a bit more and it means fatty foods aren't broken down as quickly. That's the theory of it anyway. The best thing to do is to eat healthily all the time.

EAT LIKE LIVERPOOL FC

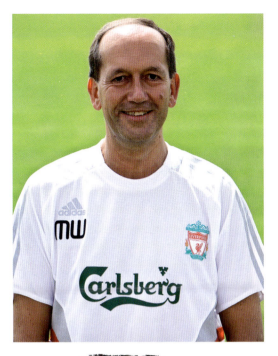

As well as helping the players prevent injuries and recover from them, Club Doctor, Mark Waller, helps them get the best out of their bodies with a diet to keep them at the top of their game

Having a good breakfast is very important

Most people involved in nutrition advice would say that breakfast is the most important meal of the day.

We advise our players that they should have cereal, fruit and maybe some low fat yoghurt and a fruit drink. Maybe orange, apple or cranberry juice. They should have their cereal with skimmed or semi-skimmed milk so that the fat content in their breakfast is low.

Some days, they might have scrambled eggs or poached eggs and some toast so that the diet is varied and doesn't become monotonous.

Sugar coated cereals are a definite no-no on a regular basis and especially on a matchday. Steer clear of any sugar on cereals.

Avoid sugar on cereals

PLAY LIKE LIVERPOOL FC

The really important day's food in any footballer's week is what you eat the day before a game

EAT LIKE LIVERPOOL FC

Being ready for morning or lunchtime kick-offs

The strange thing is, that what you eat on the day is probably less important than what you eat the day before. The really important day's food in any footballer's week is what you eat the day prior to a game. A take home message here is that what you take in an hour or two before the game, although important, is not the most important food you will eat during the week. If you eat the right foods the day before, it will be stored up in various parts of the body for you to utilise on a matchday.

If we've got a lunchtime kick-off it causes a slight problem because you can't have a full pre-match meal for breakfast because our usual pre-match meal will involve a lot of pasta, chicken and brown rice. Most players understandably don't want to eat that kind of thing at half eight in the morning so instead we go for a different pre-match meal which is based more on breakfast foods.

The right time to eat is between three and four hours before you complete the activity. At Liverpool, we tend to have it three and a half hours before if the meal is substantial.

A lot of people might wonder whether to eat before the warm-up or before the match actually starts because the warm-up usually starts 40-minutes before the start of the game. We always count it from the time when the game starts. If you leave it longer than that, players can be hungry by the time the game starts. But if you bring it closer to the kick off, players can still be full when they start running around - which is something you obviously don't want happening.

You need to eat products that are digested out of the stomach quite quickly and stored up in the body as energy. A normal breakfast with low fat yogurt and fruit usually does the trick.

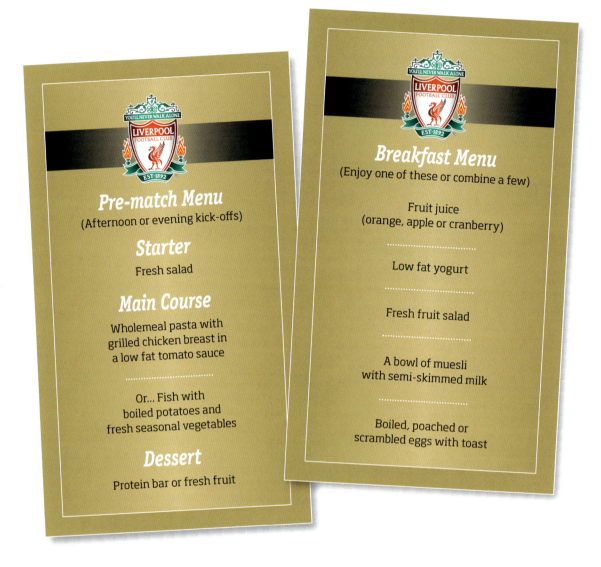

Preparing for afternoon or evening kick-offs

If we had a 3pm kick off, we'd give the players a salad starter. The majority will then have pasta – we'd recommend wholemeal pasta rather than ordinary pasta because once again, wholemeal has a lower Glycaemic index meaning you don't get a peak of sugar and carbohydrate in your blood.

Instead, you get insulin production and it leaves your system very quickly. We also encourage the players to have chicken and maybe some fish, which is full of protein. Some will have it with a simple tomato low fat sauce or maybe some brown rice. We try and mix the science and, if you like, the psychology that goes with diet because what we don't want is to be too rigid and too boring so that the food is unpleasant.

Some of our players have always had potatoes as a pre-match meal at other clubs and in other countries. We will always advise them what to do, but if they feel slightly more comfortable doing it a different way, we'll allow them to do it their way.

EAT LIKE LIVERPOOL FC

Make sure pasta sauce is low fat

Normal evening meals

We try to limit the amount of carbohydrates our players have in the evening time if they've not done a late training session. If they have, it's ok to replenish energy stores by using carbohydrates. If they haven't, however, and even if they don't have a training session the following day, in the evening time we recommend that they have protein and vegetables for their meal. In those instances, we wouldn't want them to have carbohydrates like pasta, rice and bread because if you do without the exercise, they'll probably be laid down as fats rather than muscle energy.

Every time you cook chicken or fish, you want to limit the fat content. For chicken, you'd cook a breast without the skin on it instead of a leg or the wings where there is a lot of skin and therefore more fat. Grilling, char-grilling or roasting is far more healthy than frying with a load of oil. It's the same for fish where poaching, grilling and baking is more preferable than frying, and have boiled potatoes or steamed rather than roast which are covered in fat.

Avoid snacks or eat fruit

A lot of the English players are used to eating at about five or six in the evening. Some of the non-English players wont eat until eight and usually at about nine. It's a cultural thing and what they're used to.

If you're having breakfast at eight in the morning, lunch at half 12 - 1 o'clock and dinner at 5.30, most people are going to be hungry again later on in the evening. Whereas if you eat at nine, you won't want a snack before you go to bed.

Ideally, each player will have three meals a day rather than snack. If they do, the best thing to have is protein bars or a piece of fruit. Chocolate bars and crisps are out.

Don't eat too late in the day

What you don't want to do, certainly if you're not exercising in the evening, is to have too much food later in the day. So start your day off well with proteins and carbohydrates and certainly products that have vitamins in them as well.

Drink plenty of fluids before, during and after training

The importance of fluids

Ahead of a training session, we'll always tell them to drink plenty of fluids – meaning more fruit drinks or still water.

Using more technical language, you need foods with a low Glycaemic index which means you don't want to eat foods that can be labelled as fast sugars. You need food that is broken down slowly and can be absorbed gradually. Orange juice for instance, has a high Glycaemic index so it will raise the blood sugar and energy quite quickly. Apple juice or cranberry juice, on the other hand, has a slower Glycaemic index and takes a lot longer to absorb into the body.

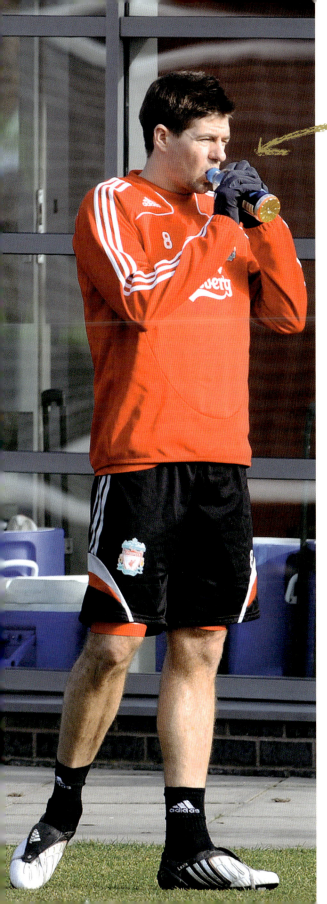

EAT LIKE LIVERPOOL FC

Get your energy levels back up within two hours

Re-fuelling

After a training session or even after a game, the most important thing to remember is that there is a two-hour window where a player can re-fuel and start preparing for the next training session or the next game. Within those two hours the regeneration of energy into the muscles is much better. If you leave it for more than two hours, it takes a longer time to get the energy levels back up to where you want them to be.

What we try to do, straight after the final whistle has been blown, is get energy drinks out to the players. If we can do that – we're then preparing them for the next game.

Once inside the dressing room, we give them more carbohydrate drinks like Lucozade which has electrolytes – similar to salts. We also give them a protein drink, which has vitamins as well as food like chicken baguettes, skewered chicken and lean ham on toast. All of the food has a very limited amount of fat.

Immediately after a game, what you're after is a source of carbohydrate. None of our players are overweight so we don't have to worry about giving them carbs. For people who already have weight, carbs might make them put more weight on.

If we've got a game on a Saturday then no games until a week on Monday and there's nine days between the games perhaps the importance of re-fuelling quickly is a lot less because there is more time to recover. If we have a game on Sunday, Wednesday and Saturday, meaning three games in six days, the importance of re-fuelling is huge because if we don't do it properly, the levels of energy and standard of performance in the second game won't be as good as it could be then in the third game it might be absolutely dreadful – especially after the first two because the players just won't have the energy.

Having said that, it doesn't mean that if you only have one game every 12 or so days you forget about re-fuelling because training is important as well as matches. So you need to link your diet in line with times of exercise and recovery.

Try to have water on hot days

During the match

Re-fuelling with fluid throughout a football match is vitally important. Particularly on a hot day you can lose three or four litres of fluid. So that means you must re-fuel after the game as well to get the balance right in your body.

Taking regular fluids during the matches is imperative and you'll regularly see us throwing drinks towards our players during breaks in play. If you feel thirsty during a game, it means you're probably already dehydrated so if you become thirsty you should drink straight away otherwise it will affect your performance.

Watch out for fizzy drinks

We don't encourage fizzy drinks. It doesn't mean that you should never have them but if you're re-fuelling or preparing for a game and have a lot of gas in your stomach you can become bloated or suffer heart-burn meaning you can't get the volume into energy levels that you need.

Some people may ask the same question about sparkling water. The same applies.

Avoiding fast food

Low fat oven chips probably have less fat than in a skinless chicken breast. Having said that, we don't want to give an impression that fast food is ok because it isn't. If you go to any fast food restaurant, the fat content is huge because they usually sell skinny chips, which are high in fat as well as fatty meat for their burgers.

Organic food is probably preferable because it's more healthy with less contaminants.

The majority of players that come to the club have a decent knowledge of nutrition. When I originally started almost 20 years ago, players' knowledge of their nutrition was nowhere near as high and neither was the club's knowledge.

Pre-season targets

Our players are given an expected weight when they return in the summer. How they achieve that weight is up to them and sometimes maybe their weight will fluctuate in a short space of time. We will take the weight a kilo or two either side of their expected weight but if they return too heavy – they will get into trouble!

The first day back in pre-season doesn't involve training. On day one, we'll do a full screening programme and we'll use all the data we receive from there to set out a plan for the next season. It's like an MOT for players.

Most important lesson

The important meals for a footballer are breakfast every day, every meal the day before a game and their intake directly after games.

PLAY LIKE LIVERPOOL FC

KEEP FIT LIKE
THE REDS

Training regularly will help you stay fit, but as well as working with the ball you will need to be able to do short sprint work and build-up stamina and endurance levels

PLAY LIKE LIVERPOOL FC

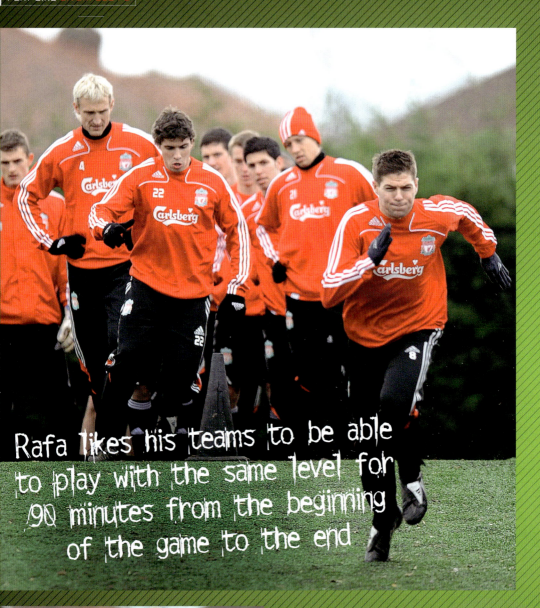

Rafa likes his teams to be able to play with the same level for 90 minutes from the beginning of the game to the end

Paco de Miguel is the man who makes sure the Liverpool players stay fit and are able to play with a high tempo for Rafa Benitez

PACO SAYS...

Keeping the players fit is the key factor in my job.

Working with the other coaches we have to make sure we have a proper plan and are pulling all the contents together.

We have to make sure all the different training sessions are ok and analyse everything to try to improve the fitness of the team.

Keeping the tempo up

Rafa pays a lot of attention to the fitness. He likes his teams to play with a high tempo, pressing when we lose the ball.

He likes his teams to be able to play with the same level for 90 minutes, from the beginning to the end. The fitness is very important to this.

Starting and ending the season strongly

Everybody is trying to start and end the season at the same level. It is one of the most difficult things to accomplish.

It is true that in our plans we work towards the whole season, not just thinking about the beginning or month by month. We work towards the whole season from start to finish.

The first three points are just as important as the last three points of the season. You can start really well but maybe finish at a medium level. Maybe that will be enough. But then perhaps you can start at a normal level but if you finish the season well you will have your chances at the end. You never know, this is why we have to keep the players as fit as possible throughout the whole season.

They have to be as fit as possible over 90 minutes as well as over the course of a full season.

Warming-up the substitutes

My main job during games is to ensure the players on the pitch are best prepared as possible. This includes those on the bench as well as the 11 starters.

We have to make sure they are ready for whenever the manager wants them. The players have to be ready to come on to the pitch in a good condition.

It is different in England than in Spain. In Spain the coaches are allowed to go on to the touchline to work with the players and get them warmed up. This isn't allowed in England. We have to stay on the bench and keep an eye on the players to make sure they are doing a proper warm-up.

KEEP FIT LIKE LIVERPOOL FC

We have an individual profile on each player so we know what areas they need to work on

Working on strengths and weaknesses with individuals

It depends on a lot of factors. One of the most important things is the individual performance of each player.

During the training sessions we try to work on an individual's strengths and weaknesses. We have an individual profile on each player so we know what areas they need to work on.

We test the players at different periods throughout the season. We can identify any weaknesses that may occur throughout the season.

For example, last season we had Sami Hyypia doing more strength and speed work than some of the other players. Sami had great stamina already so we didn't need to work on that. He needed to be quick and strong.

Sleeping and resting properly is just as important as training

For me, the training is no more than 50 per cent. The rest is really, really important.

One of the most important things is to get a proper sleep.

Some players go to bed late but we now recommend between nine and 10 O'clock as a good time if they want to get the maximum from themselves.

If they are going to sleep at 10, 11, or even after midnight it can make a massive difference.

We try to convince them how important it is to be in bed at the right time.

Another important factor is the diet. The metabolic system is very important to performance. The players need to have a proper diet. We insist they eat the right things and have a good selection of all the essential elements they need to be top sportsmen.

The third factor that is very important here is the hydration of the players. They need to be properly hydrated all day and ensure that when they wake up in the morning they have a good level of hydration.

What you eat can help with strength, speed and stamina

Normally the players' diet corresponds with the kind of training we are doing. If we are doing a lot of strength work for example - working towards strength and speed - we try to put more proteins in the diet to prepare the muscles and make sure they will recover well from this training.

If the work is focusing more on stamina we will work the other way, trying to increase the carbohydrates.

There is glycogen in the carbohydrates that are vital to replace the glycogen stores that have been lost in the muscles.

This can be done with a diet that is high in carbohydrates.

For the players to perform to the best of their ability, the performance involves everything from the club's intelligence and attitude towards fitness.

It is true that in the last 10 to 15 years the attitude has changed and there is more focus on fitness in football. Top clubs are playing more important games in close succession. This requires that the players need to be at a good level. This is why the fitness is so important.

When you are competing in the Premier League, Champions League and other competitions week after week for nine months, the recovery strategy is really important too.

The use of technology

Technology is very important to the daily work. For example, with strength work we are using a lot of devices to control the players' parameters.

We also use technology to measure the body fat and anthropometry.

Technology is useful with fitness because we can quantify everything.

It is also good for tactics through media analysis. Technology is helping football nowadays and we need to use it.

Scoring late goals

When it comes to scoring goals late in a game, like Liverpool did on a number of occasions in 2008/09, there are different factors. Sure, the fitness is one key area. If you can't arrive in the opposition's penalty area late in a game there will be no chance to score. The players must be patient. They have to play knowing that if they are patient a goal could come at any time in the 90 minutes.

If you can't arrive in the opposition's penalty area late in a game there will be no chance to score

PLAY LIKE LIVERPOOL FC

PLAY LIKE
LIVERPOOL FC

Every Liverpool fan dreams of pulling on the famous red shirt and playing at Anfield. So what are the special skills and attributes you need to help give you the best possible chance to make it happen? Let's ask the players themselves

PLAY LIKE LIVERPOOL FC

SCORE LIKE
TORRES

Liverpool's number nine is regarded by many as the greatest striker in world football. If you want to learn to play up front and score goals, learn from the best

PLAY LIKE LIVERPOOL FC

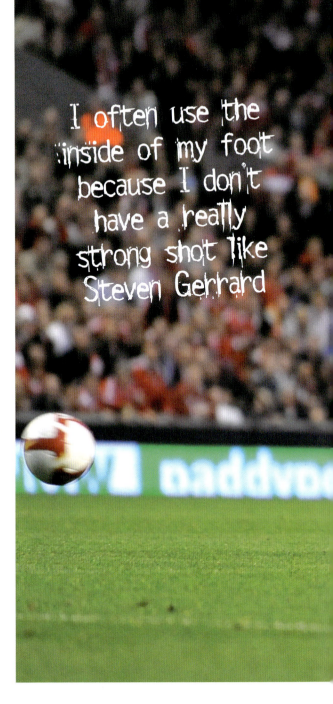

I often use the inside of my foot because I don't have a really strong shot like Steven Gerrard

FERNANDO SAYS...

I used to love hitting the ball against a wall

I see a lot of kids in Liverpool playing football. I was always playing when I was a kid too, hitting the ball against a wall or with my friends and my brother.

He was a goalkeeper so I would practice shooting against him all of the time. It is important to practice. In fact, it's not even practising. If you enjoy football, you will play as much as you can and then you will get better.

Getting your body over the ball when you shoot

It is very important and maybe even the main thing to get right.

If you learn how to position your body well over the ball it will increase your chances of scoring a goal.

The position of your body can make the difference between shooting inside the goal or missing the target.

It can also make the difference between hitting the ball along the ground or up and over the bar, which you don't want to do of course.

There are different ways to use your body. If you lean back a little bit you may be able to score in the top corner but you have to learn how to control this properly to get it right. You need a lot of training for this skill.

Going for power or accuracy

I often use the inside of my foot because I don't have a really strong shot like Steven Gerrard.

For a striker, the inside of the foot is often the best part for finishing past a goalkeeper. You can get more accuracy with the inside of the foot. But sometimes when you are outside of the box it is better to use the top of your foot to get more power.

PLAY LIKE LIVERPOOL FC

SKILL TIP...

CHIPPING THE KEEPER: Sometimes the keeper will go to ground early and when you see him do this you can try to chip the ball over him or place it to the side of him. To chip the ball you need to practise stabbing your foot under the ball to lift it slightly and get it back down so it doesn't drift over the bar.

If I am outside the box it is better to hit the ball with power sometimes

Accuracy is usually better closer to goal

As I say, I usually use the inside of the foot for accuracy. If I'm no more than three or four metres from the goal I don't really have time to prepare a hard shot.

If you are inside the area though, and manage to hit the ball accurately either side of the goalkeeper, more often than not it is a goal.

If I am outside the box it is better to hit the ball with power sometimes. If you can hit the ball between the posts with power, the goalkeeper doesn't always have time to react and make a save.

PLAY LIKE LIVERPOOL FC

SCORE LIKE TORRES

Combining power and accuracy – like my first goal against Blackburn in April 2009

Sometimes when you see the position of the goalkeeper you only have a split second to make a decision. You have to decide quickly and then be sure of what you are doing.

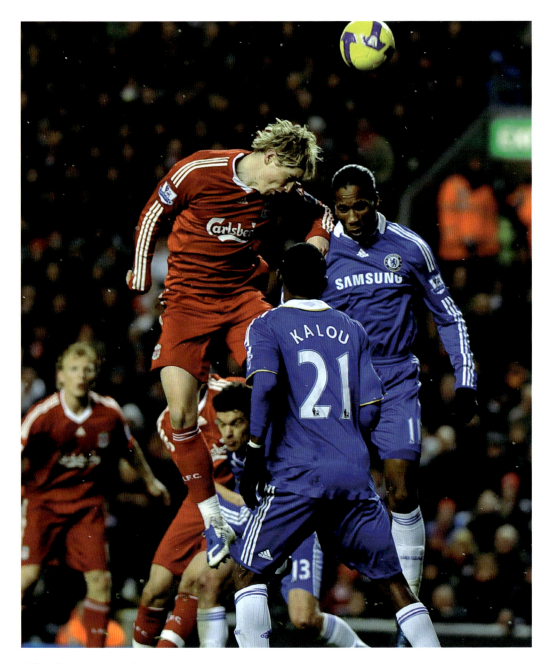

Timing your jump

The timing of your jump is very important. If you can time it right so you meet the ball with your head at the correct moment, you don't necessarily have to be a tall player to be a good header of the ball.

Luis Garcia has always been very good in the air for this reason. He isn't too tall but can time his jump well to meet the ball and also get power behind it.

The first movement when you are looking to move toward the ball to head it is very important. If you can arrive running while controlling your jump to meet the ball you will often deliver a good header, be it at goal, out of defence or to a teammate.

SCORE LIKE TORRES

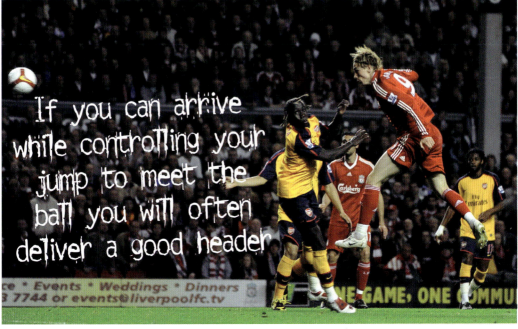

If you can arrive while controlling your jump to meet the ball you will often deliver a good header

It's not always easy keeping the ball down

Football managers will teach you that it's best to keep the ball down from a header because it makes it more difficult for goalkeepers to make a save.

That is not always possible though, especially when there are lots of people in the penalty box trying to stop you getting to the ball. Sometimes your teammates can help create space for you, such as against Blackburn in 2008/09 with my second goal.

It was good movement from Martin Skrtel to draw my marker. That allowed me to run and jump free in the correct moment. Even then I couldn't keep the ball down so instead headed it into the top corner.

It came in really quickly from Xabi Alonso's free-kick so it was difficult for me to control. Sometimes the ball hits you rather than you hitting the ball. On occasions like this you just have to get your head to it and wait and see where it ends up.

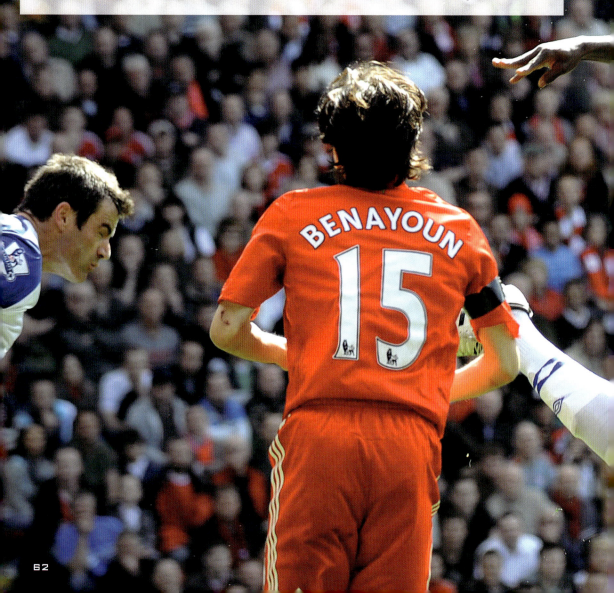

PLAY LIKE LIVERPOOL FC

Sometimes I move one way then run the other way

Quick movements can help you create a bit more space for yourself. It may just be a single step to go one way but then spinning back and running the other way.

That can be enough to get away because the defender has to stay aware of two things; the striker but also the ball.

That's what I did for my header against Blackburn. I initially moved to my right but then ran to the left. Meanwhile, the defender couldn't get past Skrtel. That gave me about one metre of space to run and jump free to head the ball in.

A goal like this always comes down to training. We had actually worked on that goal at Melwood so it was nice to see it come off in a game.

Of course, the delivery is always important too. After that you have to get the movement and the timing of the run right to give you the best chance of getting to the ball first.

Awareness for assists

Being a striker helps a great deal in terms of awareness of where a teammate will run towards goal and when to play him in. Stevie's goal at West Ham was an example of how it can work. Sometimes in football, if the defence is playing a little bit high, as West Ham were early in the game, It allowed me to control the ball but then I had to pass it at the correct moment.

A little bit later and we would have been caught offside. Had I passed it too soon, the defender may have been in a better position to get back and stop the ball running into Stevie's path.

You have to decide in a split second when and where to make the pass.

But that goal is all about Stevie's movement. He's not running straight on to the ball. Because he curved his run in a semi-circle it ensured he wasn't offside when I passed it.

Normally when you play in a team with quality like Liverpool, players like Stevie will often play between the lines. That means the opposition have to decide to stay high and try to play the offside trap or sit deep to counter our movement.

SCORE LIKE TORRES

Rafa has taught me a lot about timing my runs

It is massively important to time your run right if you don't want to get caught out by the linesman.

If you have players with a good understanding you can do a lot of things to create chances between you.

Being aware of and knowing each other's movements is part of this.

Rafa has taught me a lot about timing my runs properly. If you are a quick player with pace you can wait a little bit because you are quicker than the defender.

Players like Stevie can pass the ball perfectly so that means you don't always have to move to beat a defender. Sometimes you can find the right space and wait for them to find you with a pass that will often reach you in the perfect place. It helps to have teammates with this quality.

SCORE LIKE TORRES

Combatting strong, physical defenders

It gets more difficult every year because defenders know more about you.

The defenders in England knew me more in my second season with Liverpool than in my first. They knew my strengths and weaknesses better.

It's a two-way thing though. I got to know them better. I started to learn about the things certain defenders were better or worse at. I have to adapt depending on which defenders I am playing against.

Using the 'drag-past', which helped me score my first goal for the club

Normally I am quite comfortable with space. It means I can run and receive the ball from my teammate. Then, when a defender is waiting to see what I will do but stops, as Chelsea's Tal Ben-Haim did, it allowed me to start running again. That gave me a metre or so of space before he started running again. That was enough for me to score a goal. As soon as he stopped, I started running. Again, you have to decide in a split-second. We have a lot of time to practice these things in training. Sometimes they come up in a match, sometimes they don't. But it is good to practice everything for the moment when you can try it in a game.

PLAY LIKE LIVERPOOL FC

Running at defenders

I have already talked about how to practice making the defender stop and then starting your run as you stop him to catch him off guard and give yourself a head start to race past him.
Another way of tricking him is to drop your shoulder as though you are going to go one way and then as the defender goes to move that way to block you, you can sometimes catch him off balance and run past him the other way. Often if you can get past a defender but he is trying to run alongside you, try to keep your body between the defender and the ball, so he finds it difficult to make a tackle. It also helps if you are thinking ahead about where the goalkeeper is positioned and where your teammates are and what your next move is going to be when you get in that space.

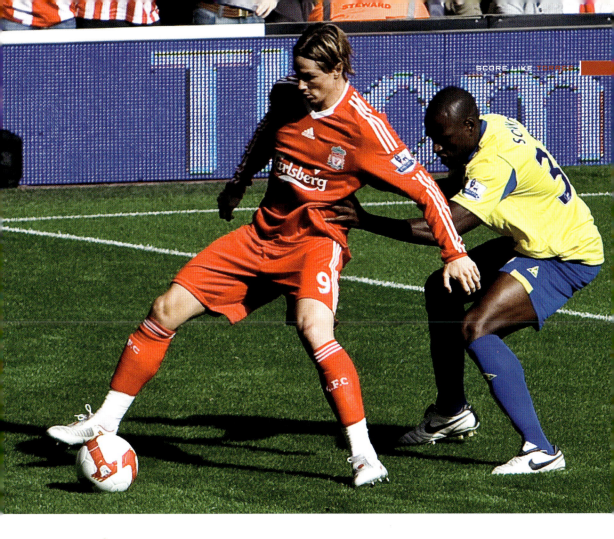

Another way of tricking a defender is to drop your shoulder as though you are going to go one way then run past him the other way

Why I think striker is the best position on the pitch

Although we are a team as 11 players in a game, the striker will have different work to some of the other players.

Defenders will often play together as a back four but strikers will sometimes operate alone up front. This is why we have time to work on individual things, often just one-on-one training with the coaches. I like the training we do as strikers because you are always working with the ball. We may be shooting at the keepers, or dribbling past defenders or moving with the ball and finishing.

It's nice work that we do in training. For me, striker is the best position on the pitch.

SCORE LIKE TORRES

I like the training we do as strikers because you are always working with the ball

Making sure you are ready when a chance comes along

Everything comes down to practice and training properly. If you want to be better you have to practice.

If you can practice four hours a day you will be better than if you practice for just one hour.

Often in games, we do things that we work on in training. A lot of the goals we score we have practised in training.

You know when your teammate is going to run somewhere. You don't even have to see him move, you know he will be there because you have practised in training.

Maybe in training I can shoot against Pepe Reina or Diego Cavalieri 20 to 30 times but it will be a different keeper in a game, maybe Petr Cech or Edwin van Der Sar. I can miss against Pepe in training and it doesn't matter. If I miss against Cech or van Der Sar in a game it does matter.

The more you practice the better you will get so that when the opportunities come along you will have a better chance of scoring when it counts in important games.

SCORE LIKE TORRES

If you can practice four hours a day you will be better than if you practice for just one hour

Looking for inspiration from your idols

I enjoyed watching my favourite players and favourite team when I was young. I would always say I would like to be like Marco van Basten or this player and that player.

I never imagined I would play football for a living. It is just a dream when you are a kid.

It is nice to get a hero though. When I was a kid mine was the Atletico Madrid striker, Kiko. He's not so famous outside of Spain but he was always my main hero.

I hoped that one day I might be able to play with him, which I was fortunate enough to do. But as a kid it was just a dream. It wasn't a real target and there was no pressure from my family or anything like that, which is important.

I just kept playing, enjoying and practising with my friends. The main thing was that I enjoyed playing football.

Playing at Anfield

I feel very comfortable at Anfield. I feel at home there.

It's hard to explain I just feel very at ease playing on that ground. It's been like that from day one.

For some reason a lot of my goals there have come in front of the Kop.

It just felt good from the start. I am very happy playing and scoring goals there. You try more things when you feel more relaxed.

Sometimes you just can't explain why you feel particularly good in a certain place but that is what has happened to me at Anfield.

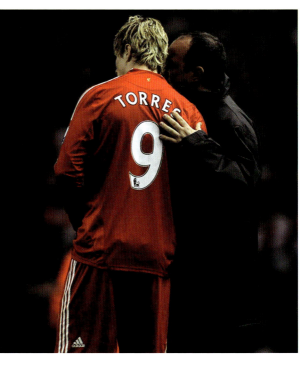

Working as a team to win trophies

Scoring goals is what I do.

It's all part and parcel of what I do as a footballer.

But I didn't come to Liverpool and make it a priority to score a certain amount of goals. I never put an actual figure on things.

What's important is the group and the team as a whole. I came here to win trophies. That is a target we are all trying to achieve.

The goals come as a result of team work and working together. It is great that I score goals and the more the better.

But, as I say, my main objective is to win titles.

Everyone in the team has a job. It is the job of the strikers to score goals but everyone has their own important function. It is all about team work.

Although it is what I do for a living, playing football and scoring goals never feels like a job.

It never becomes like that for me. I feel fortunate that I am able to do something I love so much.

I never wake up in the morning and think 'oh no, I have training today.'

I love training and love playing football. You never get used to that feeling. It is not something that ever becomes ordinary.

PLAY LIKE LIVERPOOL FC

LEAD LIKE
GERRARD

Every team needs a leader, an inspirational captain to lift those around him. Steven Gerrard went from the streets of Huyton to the leader of Liverpool Football Club. Here's how he did it

PLAY LIKE LIVERPOOL FC

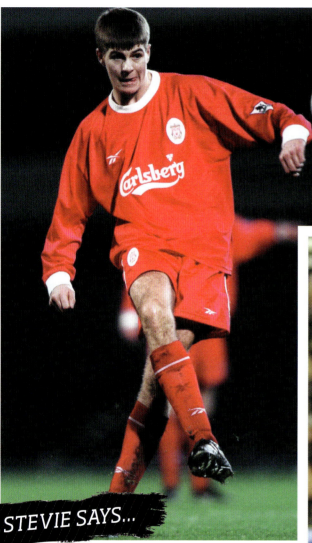

STEVIE SAYS…

Learning your trade

I used to play football all the time on the streets in Huyton and get kicked from pillar to post by the older boys.

That sort of education for a footballer is priceless. It was one of those places where you didn't complain about it, you just picked yourself up and got on with it. It certainly toughened me up and I think those lessons have helped me right throughout my career.

Coming from a council estate and growing up battling with the older lads and not really having too much as a kid definitely gave me a hunger to succeed at the very top level.

Be versatile

Over the course of my career at Liverpool I've played just about everywhere. I've played right-back, all across the midfield and I've played further forward too. As a young player trying to break through, it always helps your case for selection if you're able to play in more than one position.

Me when I was a youngster at Liverpool

Don't be put off by setbacks

Years ago I had absolutely no confidence in my body being able to play 50 or 60 games a season.

It really used to get me down and there were times when, naturally, you wonder whether you'll ever be able to stay fit long enough to become a regular. Those days now are thankfully long gone.

In the past three or four years everything's come together for me, and I feel great. You are always wary of getting carried away, but I train every day the same as the rest of the lads and it's very, very rare for me to ever miss a session. That simply wasn't the way it used to be.

I just didn't think it was possible because of the problems I had with my body when I was growing up. It was an incredibly frustrating time for me and every time I felt I was starting to get back to full fitness I would break down again.

But with hard work and belief I've got to where I wanted to be.

PLAY LIKE LIVERPOOL FC

Shoot like me

Technique's something that everyone can work on throughout their career.

No-one is born with the perfect technique, you learn and improve all the time as you go along and its one of those things that gets better the more you practice.

But when I was a kid I always had a ball at my feet and I was always knocking it about. If there was no-one around then I'd just be hitting shots at a wall myself. You don't need to be playing in a game to improve your skills.

I used to spend hours and hours as a kid trying to hit targets with shots from different angles and distances and it does help you.

It doesn't matter how much talent or ability you're born with, if you don't work hard on improving then you won't get to where you want to be. Not just in football but in any part of life. Nothing worth having comes easily.

LEAD LIKE GERRARD

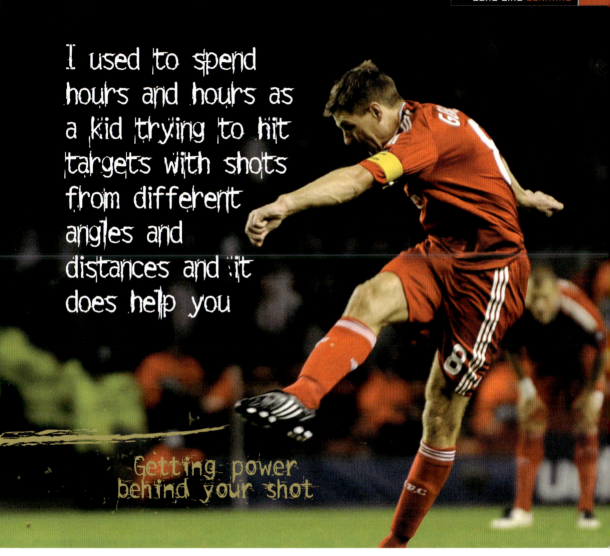

I used to spend hours and hours as a kid trying to hit targets with shots from different angles and distances and it does help you

Getting power behind your shot

PLAY LIKE LIVERPOOL FC

As you can see even Steven Gerrard can get get it wrong. Here, against Atletico Madrid he gets underneath the ball and sends it high over the bar

SKILL TIP...

VOLLEYS: Shooting on the volley is a tough skill to master but when you get it right it can result in some stunning goals.

Keeping your eye on the ball is absolutely crucial as you line the ball up.

Balance yourself by using your arms and then you need to imagine where the ball is going to drop for you to hit it.

Plant your non-kicking foot into the turf, steady yourself and keep your head still as you focus on the ball - even if an opponent is challenging you.

Lead from your knee as you bring your leg through and try to strike the centre or top of the ball with your instep.

Your leg should be bent slightly with your toes pointing down but if you bring your leg through too quickly you'll struggle to control your shot.

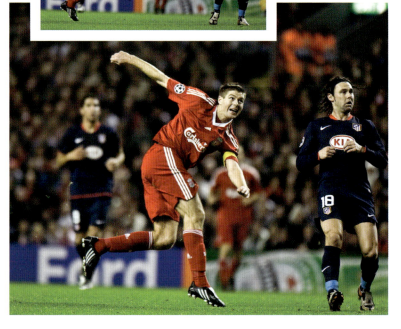

LEAD LIKE GERRARD

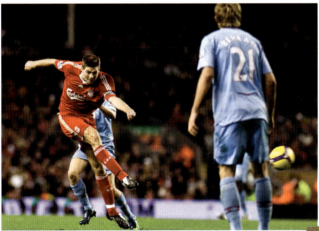

SKILL TIP...

GETTING POWER INTO YOUR SHOTS: Striking the ball with power makes it harder to direct if you don't get your technique right.

To get power you need to strike the ball with your instep and bring your kicking leg through quickly.

Again, use your arms for balance and for extra power lift your standing leg off the ground as part of your follow-through.

However, if you don't get your head over the ball and focus on it then your shot will be heading into the Kop rather than the net.

Low shots are harder for goalkeepers to save as they have further to travel to get down to the ground so if you get your power and accuracy right when striking the ball, the chances are that you'll score.

As ever, regularly practising your technique is a must.

PLAY LIKE LIVERPOOL FC

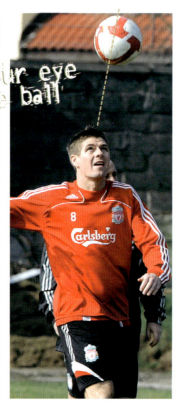

Keep your eye on the ball

SKILL TIP...

CONCENTRATE AT ALL TIMES: Wherever the ball is, and whether you are training or playing, always keep your eye on it. That may sound obvious but lapses of concentration can be very costly in football so even when you are training you need to get into good habits to prepare you for matchday.

To improve your concentration and co-ordination, see how long you can balance the ball on your head without it dropping to the ground.

Balance

LEAD LIKE GERRARD

SKILL TIP...

WORK ON YOUR CONTROL: If you can't control the ball then you won't be able to use your other skills so practice cushioning it with your instep, outstep, chest, thigh and head until you have it mastered.

Now see if you can cushion the ball so it lands in front of you and sets you up to pass or shoot with your second touch.

Trying it while a mate attempts to win the ball off you is even better as that will prepare you for trying to control the ball when put under pressure during a match.

Cushion the ball with your chest

PLAY LIKE LIVERPOOL FC

SKILL TIP...

BURSTING FROM MIDFIELD: If you've received the ball in the centre of the park and you've got space to run into, bursting forward from midfield can be a superb option.

Defenders don't like players running at them and if a centre-half has to move forward from the back line to try and stop you then it can create space for your teammates to run into.

If you do drive forward from midfield then using the ball well at the end of your run is vital.

Should the defence back off, the chance to shoot from long range will open up but if an opponent comes towards you then it's a case of selecting the right pass to make to a teammate.

One thing you shouldn't do is try to beat every man yourself.

You are more likely to get tackled than skip past three or four defenders and losing possession too often will annoy your teammates and infuriate your manager.

If you really don't have a pass on then attempting to dribble through on your own might be your only option but if you're playing against a half-decent team then that will be incredibly difficult to do.

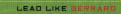

PASSING FROM CENTRE MIDFIELD:
If you're playing in a central position you are closer to everyone else on the pitch and can be used as an outlet as well as being the player who is always looking for other teammates.

Because of that you have to get the ball and assess where your teammates are and look for the best option.

It's just as important to find space after you've made the pass so that you are available for your teammates again.

PLAY LIKE LIVERPOOL FC

Listen to good advice

I'm being helped now knowing where I'm going to be playing week-in and week-out. The manager and the coaches tell me what I do right and what I do wrong in this position and make sure that I learn from my mistakes. They push me for consistency.

I'm in a position now where I'm always confident I can cause other teams problems. I can get into the box to score goals, I can go wide and create chances for other lads and I can get back and help out with the defensive duties when we're under pressure.

Conquering nerves

Personally, in the Champions League final in Istanbul, everything was new for me and it took its toll. Everyone was talking about the history this club has in the European Cup and our previous successes and we felt a bit of pressure on us to emulate some of their achievements.

I know I wasted a lot of energy with nerves before the game but I won't make the same mistakes again. I can't speak for the rest of the boys from 2005 but I'm sure they felt the same pressures as me and it had the same effect on them.

When you're nervous you get tight, you don't make the right decisions and you don't play to the best of your ability. Having a few nerves are important before the game, but we had too many in the team in 2005 and I think it probably showed in the first 45 minutes. It was only really when we were staring down the barrel of the gun at half-time that we started to play anything like ourselves.

We didn't do ourselves justice in the first half in Istanbul. The comeback was incredible, something no-one who was there, or saw it on TV will ever forget, but we shouldn't have been in that position in the first place. We were a better side in 2005 than we showed on the night.

Setting standards

I've spoken about how you have to be honest with yourself. The only way that can happen is by taking responsibility for yourself and your performances. Going away from games, going home at night and looking at the league table I think you have to realise that you're not doing your job properly if Liverpool are in a bad position.

The team can't function unless individuals are functioning fully. That's the first thing. I have to sort my own form out and there are other players in our dressing room who have to do the same as me. I'm sure we see better team performances when that happens and you've got to continue to keep doing the right things, keep working hard in training and keep working hard in games.

You don't get anything in football, or any walk of life, without hard work and we've got to remember that. Our success under Rafa Benitez has been built on it, and that's the only way we'll be successful in the future. The difficult thing for me is that I've set standards for myself where people expect top, top performances from me week-in and week-out. That's good, I'd rather play with that type of expectation around me, than not, but when I fall a little bit below that standard people are very quick to notice it, and point it out.

If it's not happening then you don't go home and stand in front of a mirror and pull your hair out. That doesn't help. You watch your games on the television, I always record them for that reason, and you see where you're going wrong. Those are the only ways I know to put things right.

PLAY LIKE LIVERPOOL FC

You're playing in a big match that your team desperately needs to win when the ref points to the penalty spot. The responsibility to hit the net lies with you. How do you handle the pressure? How do you calm the nerves? How do you beat the keeper?

LEAD LIKE GERRARD

I used to miss penalties because of the fear factor

I've got more confident the more I've taken. I think that's just a natural thing as you mature. Missing doesn't ever enter my thoughts now.

I used to miss the odd pen here and there because I was frightened. I'd beat myself before I'd hit it.

I've grown into taking pens and I always feel as if I'm going to score. I wouldn't be hitting them otherwise.

The best penalty advice I could give would be to never change your mind about where you're going to put it.

I actually changed my mind about where I was going to put my penalty against Real Madrid at Anfield as I got to the end of my run up. That's not something I ever normally do and I'd definitely advise against it.

Normally I've made up my mind where I'm going to put it before I even spot the ball.

I'd had some advice from our Spanish lads before the match in case we got a penalty.

Casillas is good facing pens and they warned me to keep it low and make sure there was plenty of pace on the shot.

So that's what I intended to do, and I'd actually set my mind on putting it to the side he went for.

But as I started my run up, I was watching him closely and he made up his mind really early so I went the other way. But it's not something I'll get into the habit of doing.

LEAD LIKE GERRARD

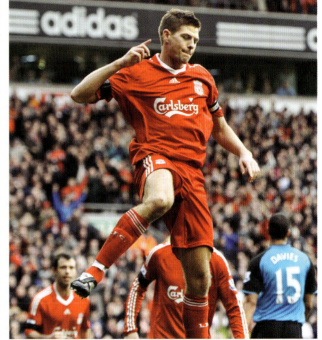

PLAYING ON THE WINGS LIKE RIERA

ALBERT SAYS...

Beating your man

There is no best way to beat your opponent every single time. It doesn't matter at what level you are playing at – charity games or Champions League – if you always try to beat your man in the same manner then he will read your intentions and counter you.

Variation in your game is important in every position, but it's essential on the wing where I play.

You have to mix-up your moves. If you dribble past your man on his outside the first time, then you can try it again. But you should also look to go the other way and beat him inside so that he cannot anticipate which direction you're going to take.

Don't be predictable

Also, you don't have to try and beat your man every time. Sometimes, a simple pass to a teammate is the best way of advancing up field rather than trying to dribble the ball half the length of the field.

If there is a teammate in a better position than you are, then use him.

The ball can move quicker than even the fastest player so it is important not to always treat the ball as yours.

PLAYING ON THE WINGS LIKE RIERA

You don't have to try and beat your man every time

SKILL TIP...

DIFFERENT CROSSES: There are different ways of crossing a ball after you have beaten your man.

Powerfully driven low crosses into your opponents' penalty area - particularly on the edge of the six yard box - are notoriously hard to defend.

Such a cross creates uncertainty between the goalkeeper and his defenders as to who should take responsibility and there's always a chance of a lucky deflection going into the net.

If a winger has a big striker to aim for, or an attacking mifielder who times his runs late, then a chipped cross to the centre of the penalty area or far post can be most effective.

Another option, particularly when in a deeper wide position, is to cross the ball early before even taking on the full-back.

A good first touch to cushion the ball in front of you, before attempting to curl the ball around your marker but so it arcs away from the goal.

This gives a striker the chance to attack your cross and may even draw the goalkeeper off his line and into no-man's land.

PLAYING ON THE WINGS LIKE RIERA

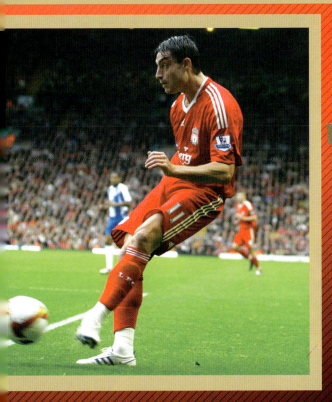

SKILL TIP...

GET YOUR HEAD UP: Crossing the ball isn't just about aimlessly hitting it into the box but picking out a teammate.

As you can see from these pictures, Albert Riera sometimes crosses with his head up.

Rather than look at the ball, he's looking for the teammate his is aiming for and that technique allows him to cross with precision.

In the pictures above he is drilling the ball across the penalty area and in that instance his focus is on the ball as he tries to put as much power behind it as possible.

To cross the ball low then you must lean over it but to float the ball into the box then it's a case of leaning back slightly to get some backlift.

Getting the correct bodyshape and striking the ball at the right angle are important if the cross is to be accurate.

Lean back too much and you're in danger of over-hitting it, strike it hard without looking and the chances are that you'll simply hit the first man.

Practice getting to the byline and trying to pick out a mate while another friend tries to intercept it.

PLAY LIKE LIVERPOOL FC

SKILL TIP...

BETWEEN THE LINES: For attacking midfielders like Yossi Benayoun, playing 'between the lines' is an important discipline to master.

If your manager asks you to play between the lines then it means he wants you to operate in the area between the opposition's defence and midfield.

An attacking midfielder playing in that role can be particularly difficult to mark as often a centre-half will be attracted to him, breaking the defensive line.

By pulling a centre-back out of position it creates space for teammates to run into so anyone playing between the lines must be good on the ball, have quick feet in order to beat a defensive midfield marker and show intelligent movement.

The ability to play first-time passes, particularly one-twos, is vital, while such players must also be able to play accurate through passes for strikers to latch on to as they will regularly find themselves in space in attacking areas.

A lot of those qualities are found in wingers so some managers will ask a wide player to play in a central position between the lines.

Benayoun is a fine example of a player who is not only comfortable playing in both roles but also contributes goals.

PLAY LIKE LIVERPOOL FC

SKILL TIP...

GETTING GOALS FROM WIDE POSITIONS: Scoring goals as well as creating them is an aspect of a winger's game that must not be overlooked.

A successful team needs goals from every area of the pitch and those playing out wide have to make a contribution.

Ryan Babel has weighed in with his fair share of goals and the fact he is a right-footed winger who often plays on the left has been a contributory factor as he will cut inside his man and attempt to curl the ball around the goalkeeper.

Shooting across the keeper is important as even if he manages to get a hand to the ball, he may only push it out to a teammate who is lurking in front of goal.

A winger must also ensure that he gets himself into the box at the far post when the ball is on the other flank in an attacking area.

Doing so gives the man on the opposite wing an extra target to aim at and ensures there is someone in position to take advatage if a defender or goalkeeper goes for the cross and misses it.

Babel was in the right place at the right time to get this goal at West Ham and he also scored a winner against Manchester United by getting himself into the penalty area to meet a loose ball.

It's all about decision-making when you're a winger.

PLAYING ON THE WINGS LIKE BABEL

STOP THE OPPOSITION LIKE
MASCHERANO

STOP THE OPPOSITION LIKE MASCHERANO

To win a game you need to win the ball. The role of midfield enforcer is vital in the modern day game and few are better at it than Liverpool and Argentina's midfield chief Javier Mascherano

Timing your tackles right

Don't just dive into a tackle. When you are young, the first instinct is to simply throw yourself into the tackle whenever you see the ball.

But the most important part of making a tackle is choosing the correct time to commit to getting the ball, and that is not always the first chance you get.

You need to get your body into the right position first of all so that when you go to get the ball you don't get the player as well.

No matter how good your opponent is with the ball at his feet there is always going to be a moment when they make a mistake. Often, this will be simply putting the ball too far in front of them and that is the time you choose to make your tackle.

You must be patient making tackles. You cannot just dive in all the time because you're not always going to get it right. In fact, you will get it wrong more times than you get it right.

Try to stay on your feet as often as possible

The other useful advice I could offer on tackling is not to go off your feet if you can avoid it. You should only make your tackle a slide tackle if it is the last resort.

Because if you go down and miss the tackle then you have no chance to recover and make another tackle.

You are out of the game if you're lying on your back and your opponent has run away from you.

If you stay on your feet then you have the chance to make up ground even if you don't quite get the ball where you want it to be. You can have a second chance to get it right.

The other thing is that if you get a slide tackle wrong then you are risking a card from the referee because sliding fouls always appear worse to a referee than a tackle when you are on your feet.

Once you have been booked then making more tackles in the game becomes much more dangerous because you are walking a tightrope.

Whenever you can stay on your feet.

STOP THE OPPOSITION LIKE MASCHERANO

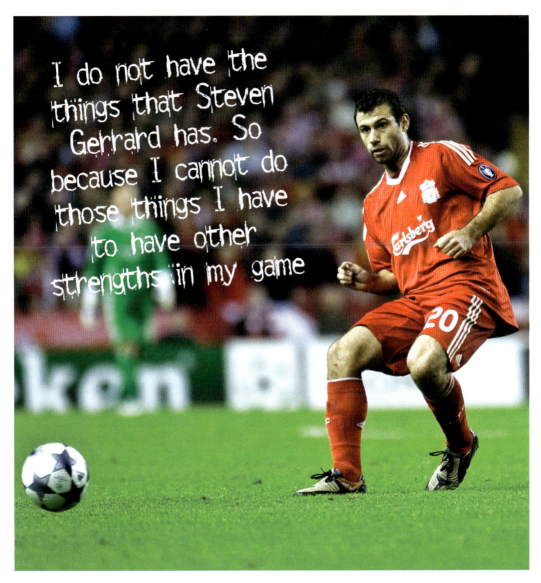

I do not have the things that Steven Gerrard has. So because I cannot do those things I have to have other strengths in my game

Play to your strengths

I do not have the things that Steven Gerrard has. He is a wonderful footballer and can beat players by doing movements and with pace that I will never have. I wish I did, sometimes, but I don't. So because I cannot do those things I have to have other strengths in my game. Of course, I always try to play football the right way and to help the team any way I can. If I see a pass then I will try it. I have the confidence to attempt things but they won't come off for me as often as they will for the other midfielders.

You must strive to improve your game every day

Steven Gerrard is one of the best midfielders in the world - maybe even the very best.

He can do everything and yet every day in training and in the matches he is trying to be better. He always wants to improve.

That is one of the things we share because I am always watching the others and listening to my managers because I know that I too can keep getting better.

I am playing well for Liverpool because I enjoy the way this team plays, but that does not mean that there are not ways and areas where I can go from 90 per cent to 95 per cent. Then later I try to get to 100 per cent.

You must always strive to improve your game, every single day of your professional life. You can never be happy with your form because there are always things that you can do better.

STOP THE OPPOSITION LIKE MASCHERANO

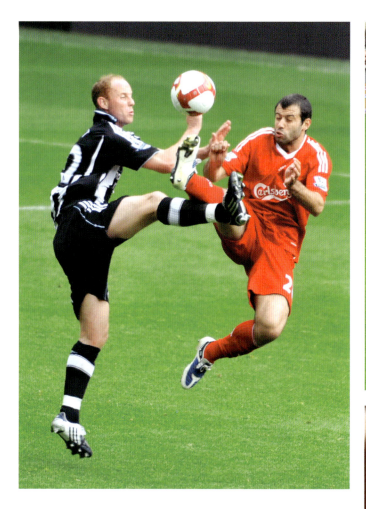

I believe that determination can overcome size

I am not as tall as Steven Gerrard, or even as tall as many of the players that I play against. So I need to be brave and prove for every minute of every game that I have a big heart.

I would say that in my position, because of my size, I have to try twice as hard as the opposition players I am playing against.

I am the smallest player in the Liverpool team. I am maybe one of the smallest central midfielders in the country and people will, I am sure, look at me before we play them and think that they will be able to dominate me physically.

I think that in the course of my time at Liverpool I have proved that they can't. I won't let them.

Sometimes it is hard. When you have to challenge for headers with people who are almost twice the height that you are and in 50/50 challenges when they bring several stones more into the tackle.

That is why when I am asked who the toughest players are to play against for me in England I cannot choose one over the other.

Skilled midfielders playing for the top clubs are tough opponents for everyone to play against. However, playing against Derby or Reading can be just as hard for me because their players can be big and strong.

But I try my best, like I always do. I never pull out of a tackle and I think that commitment and determination overcome my size.

If I can do it, then everyone can do it. Believe you are strong enough to tackle, believe you can win the ball in every situation and never be afraid even if the person is twice your size.

STOP THE OPPOSITION LIKE MASCHERANO

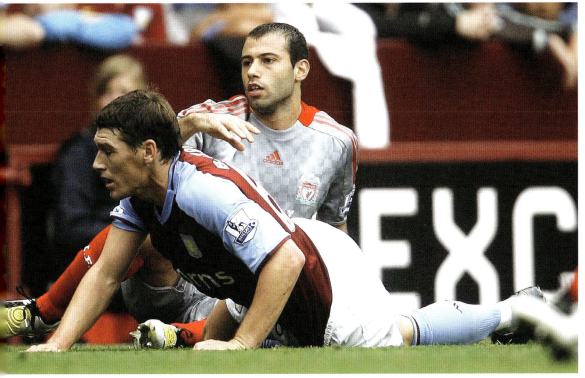

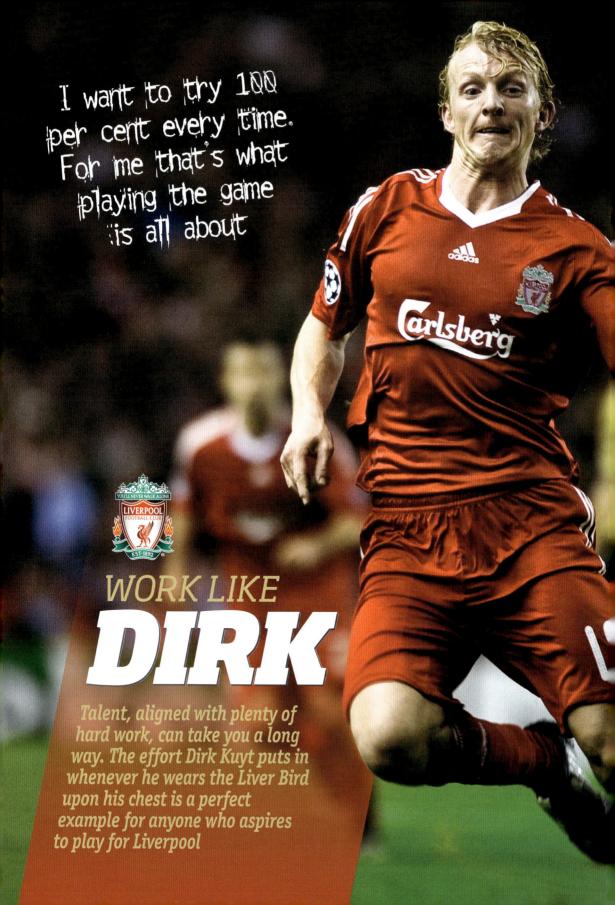

WORK LIKE DIRK

DIRK SAYS...

Ever since I was a kid, I've always tried my hardest

I always try to give my best for the team, the supporters and the club.

I want to try 100 per cent every time. For me that's what playing the game is all about. If I don't do that I don't feel like I've worked properly.

Every game I play I always have that attitude. Ever since I was a kid and started playing football I've been like that.

I always want to win and try my hardest to do so. I think that's just the way I am.

I don't think I was ever coached to be like that it's just natural.

I don't know where my energy comes from, I don't eat anything special or have any secret.

Chasing the opposition around the field and constantly pressuring defenders can get frustrating, particularly if they are passing the ball around you all the time.

But if you can regain possession from them, even just once, that helps your team, gives the fans a lift and makes life easier.

PLAY LIKE LIVERPOOL FC

Hard work is for every member of the team

At Liverpool everybody has that responsibility. We all put the other team under pressure all over the pitch and make it hard for them. That's what you have to do when you don't have the ball.

WORK LIKE DIRK

Even when a situation looks bad, never give up

The rewards for never giving up

Refusing to quit, even when a match looks lost is important for every team.

In my time at the club we've done it lots, especially in the 2008/09 campaign.

We found ourselves in losing positions against Middlesbrough, Man United twice, Marseille, Man City, Wigan and Portsmouth before going on to win.

Each time we continued to work hard and battled our way back into the game.

Those victories are great examples of what hard work can do for a player and the team, even when a situation looks bad. You can never give up.

WORK LIKE DIRK

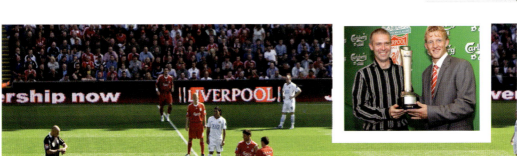

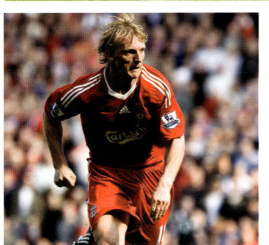

How to cope without your best players

Having your best players missing is part of football. However the mentality of our team is always strong enough to fight whenever those situations occur.

If Fernando or Stevie are absent the rest of us just work that bit harder to get a result.

PLAY LIKE LIVERPOOL FC

DEFEND LIKE CARRA

DEFEND LIKE
CARRA

He leads from the back, never shirks a tackle, organises his team-mates and will give anything for a clean sheet. Jamie Carragher is the ultimate defender's defender

JAMIE SAYS...

Be proud to be a defender

Defending is an art just like attacking or playing in midfield. It's also the position where you get the least credit. It's not the most glamorous position on a football pitch.

But it's an important role, and in the modern game you can still get involved in starting moves and creating goals too.

It's not like it used to be where defenders just defend. That's your first job, your most important one, but you've got to get comfortable with the ball at your feet.

PLAY LIKE LIVERPOOL FC

Teamwork is the key to defending, don't do it all on your own

At Liverpool, we take as much pleasure from a clean sheet as we do from great goals. We defend as a team, from the forwards all the way back to Pepe Reina.

That's one of the most important lessons for any team to take on. It's not just your defence that defend. You need that help from all over the pitch.

If your team's not losing goals then your chances of winning games are going to improve. If you're solid at the back then you only need one chance and one goal to win games.

DEFEND LIKE CARRA

At Liverpool we take as much pleasure from a clean sheet as we do from great goals

DEFEND LIKE CARRA

Don't dive in

The most important thing when tackling is anticipating when to make the challenge. A lot of kids dive in to tackle when really they should try and stay on their feet and wait for the right moment to either go to ground or put their foot in. There are times when you must make the choice to make the tackle early, but the ability to do that properly comes when you develop anticipation. Whenever you make a tackle, it's important to make sure you get your whole body weight behind you and make sure you remain strong. That way, you're more than likely going to come away with the ball as well as making sure you don't get injured. I've seen some bad injuries when players go in half-hearted.

Positioning and understanding your teammates

Positioning is something a defender can work hard on and develop over the years. Although it comes naturally to some people, it's an attribute that can be worked on and improved if you put the time in on the training ground. If you're a centre half like me, it's important to have an understanding with your partner at the back as well as the full-backs and the defensive minded midfielder, whereas if you're a full-back, you need to understand when to break forward and when to stay back in-line with the winger in front of you. It's also important to have a good on-field relationship with the keeper – then you can judge when to let things pass through to him and when to clear the ball.

Positioning is something that can be worked on and improved if you put the time in

Playing the offside trap

Executing an offside trap properly can only happen when you develop a good understanding with the defenders around you. Again, the offside trap is linked to positioning because you must be aware of the players around you as well as your own movement to make sure you get it right, otherwise, the opposition forwards are going to get in behind you. An offside trap is also dependent on whether the manager wants to employ one. Some defences have more pace so it's easier to play that way, then other defences have less pace, so they prefer to defend deeper – especially when they are facing a forward line that's fast.

DEFEND LIKE CARRA

You must be aware of the players around you as well as your own movement

DEFEND LIKE CARRA

Getting the basics right

I play footy with my own kids in the garden. My lad doesn't really have a position on the pitch yet - that should come when he gets a bit older. I was a striker when I was a kid and now, I think some people find that hard to believe.

I always tell my son to keep his balance with his arms out when on the ball and when trying to tackle, keep his eyes on the ball and stay on his feet without diving in. It's important never to lose sight of the basics.

PLAY LIKE LIVERPOOL FC

DEFEND LIKE AGGER

DEFEND LIKE AGGER

Defending isn't just about tackling. A bit of class and composure on the ball at the back can take a team up a level. Fancy yourself as a ball-playing centre-half? Dan's the man to learn from

It is a big pitch and you want to try and stretch your opponents to create space

DANIEL SAYS...

Bringing the ball out from the back

I'm never going to be a player who simply defends. When I have won the ball back I always think about going forward and linking the play.

That is how I have been able to score some goals in my career. Young players should be brave and take the chance. Some coaches don't want their defenders to do it but I think if your centre-back can bring the ball out of defence then it can open up spaces further forward for midfielders and forwards.

It is a big pitch, and you want to try and stretch your opponents to create space.

Football would be a less exciting sport if people did not take risks in the game. That's what you need to do in defence sometimes when you bring the ball forward.

You learn more from your mistakes than your successes

You need to learn when to take the calculated gamble and bring the ball forward. Sometimes you will lose the ball, that's normal, but other times you will be able to have an influence on the game. That's a great thing to do as a defender.

Look at Liverpool, Carra will bring the ball forward when he can. So will Martin Skrtel and myself too I think. I like to play football. It is something that we are encouraged to do.

Young players should be brave and express themselves. You will make mistakes, of course, that is only normal.

But you learn more from your mistakes than you do from your successes and when that happens you will be able to decide better when the opportunity is there to play football from defence, or when you should just clear your lines.

Sometimes you just have to get the ball away, and it's important to learn as early as you can when to play and when not to.

DEFEND LIKE AGGER

Getting comfy on the ball

I played in just about every position on the football pitch. I started life as a striker and I did okay in the forward positions.

I scored some goals and made some goals and that's your job in that position.

Then a little later I moved one step backwards into the midfield and I enjoyed playing there too. You can tackle and really get involved in the physical side of the game in that position but you see a lot of the ball and you can play passes and get forward also.

That was one of the best things about my footballing education, I got to learn a lot in a number of different positions. It allowed me to become comfortable on the ball, you learn what you can do in possession and when and how to make the right type of passes.

If you can, it is a great thing to do, rather than simply specialising in the one position.

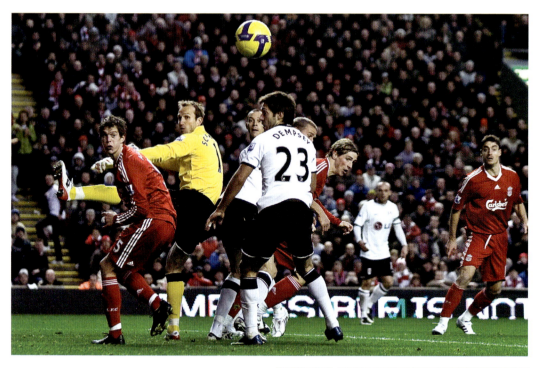

Being flexible will help you

Eventually, my coaches came to me and asked me if I would play in central defence. I wasn't the tallest player in the team but they had seen something in the way I tackled that made them think I would work well in this position.

I think I was the most aggressive person in the team in the challenge and they wanted to harness that ability in defence.

I was happy to do that, but even now I think with training I think I could still play striker or midfield or in the full-back positions. The more flexible you can be as a player the better it will be for you in the long run.

DEFEND LIKE AGGER

> I think I was the most aggressive person in the team in the challenge and they wanted to harness that ability in defence

PLAY LIKE LIVERPOOL FC

DEFEND LIKE
SKRTEL

*Bravery. Guts. Commitment. Power. No fear.
Martin Skrtel isn't a man that opponents mess with*

> Sometimes you have to put your body on the line to prevent an oppostion player scoring a goal

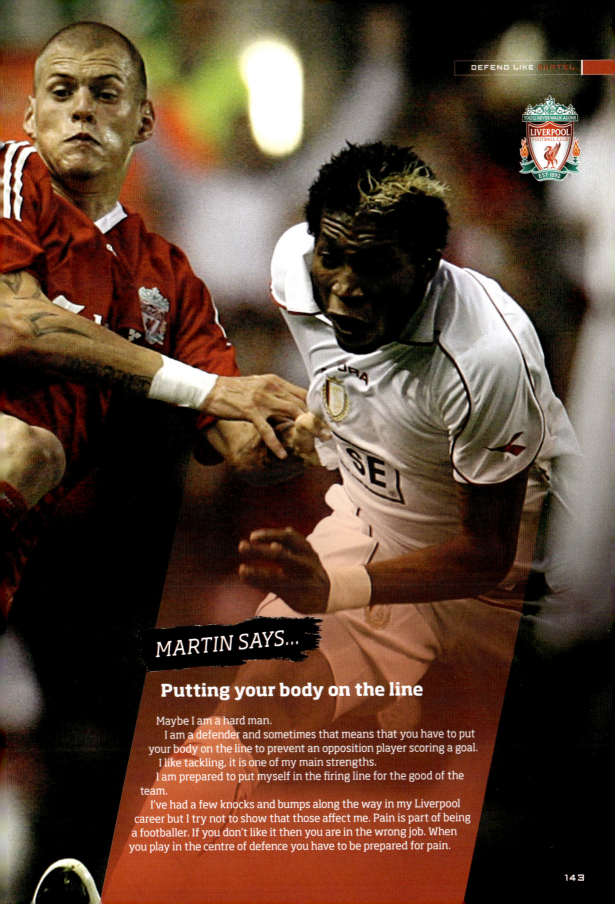

DEFEND LIKE SKRTEL

MARTIN SAYS...

Putting your body on the line

Maybe I am a hard man.

I am a defender and sometimes that means that you have to put your body on the line to prevent an opposition player scoring a goal.

I like tackling, it is one of my main strengths.

I am prepared to put myself in the firing line for the good of the team.

I've had a few knocks and bumps along the way in my Liverpool career but I try not to show that those affect me. Pain is part of being a footballer. If you don't like it then you are in the wrong job. When you play in the centre of defence you have to be prepared for pain.

Make life tough

I am not in the team to make life easy for strikers. If I was doing that I don't think I would be playing.

My job is to keep them from scoring goals, any way that I can.

It's true that I am a physical player. I think I am strong enough to match up to any striker but I am also fair.

I don't try and make it a personality battle.

One of the keys to winning football matches is to win the battles between the players; like centre back against centre forward or central midfielder against central midfielder.

But I try not to make it a battle of personalities.

Aim for the very top

I do not like losing. I hate losing, and that is an attitude I always take with me onto the football field.

Perhaps growing up where I did had something to do with my mentality, my outlook on life. I always wanted more than I had in my hometown. I always wanted to leave it behind and make my way in the wider world.

From a very young age growing up back home in Slovakia I wanted to be a footballer.

Playing football gave me the chance of a way out of my village. It is a coal mining region, very industrial, and there are few bright career

DEFEND LIKE SKRTEL

Listen to your teammates

You look at Jamie Carragher's level, his consistency of performance, and there might not be anyone better.

We have a lot of great players at the club but he is one of the very best.

In football terms I am still young, so I am still learning about positions and tactics all the time. I watch and listen to what Jamie says and I try to learn from him.

We have formed a good partnership, just as Sami Hyypia and Daniel Aggger have been able to forge great partnerships with Jamie.

He is the one constant in the defence and it is easy to understand why.

Like me he hates losing. You can see it on his face in every tackle.

He talks me through games, and he leads by his example. He hates making mistakes, and hates us making mistakes too. If you do make mistakes, then he will let you know all about it.

I have made them in games, maybe not huge ones that have cost us goals or points but I have made them. Maybe it is having Jamie alongside me, covering for me, that they have not proved costly.

prospects back home.

Things are better now than they were when I was growing up but those conditions, for me, made it vital to me to get away.

I worked hard every day, in every training session, to improve and get better and take my chance.

Doing what I am doing now is a dream come true. I have left home behind and I am playing for one of the world's biggest and best football clubs. I got here because I have determination, because I don't give up easily and because I am prepared to work hard to get what I want.

ATTACK FROM THE BACK LIKE JOHNSON

GLEN SAYS...

You have to know when to defend and when to attack

As a right-back, I love to get forward. It's something I do naturally and I think it's an important thing for full-backs to do.

I also think it's important for an attacking full-back to get a few goals during a season and get as many assists as possible.

Obviously, you also have to be able to defend and work as part of a defensive line and it's ideal if you are versatile enough to play at right or left-back.

Good stamina levels are vital as there is a lot of running to do, up and down the line, and you need to be able to pass accurately as full-back is a position that tends to see a lot of the ball.

You also need to time your forward runs as constantly bombing forward from full-back will leave your team vulnerable to counter-attacks.

Having a midfielder in front of you who you can be sure will cover when you attack is a plus as it means you can get forward with confidence.

PLAY LIKE LIVERPOOL FC

KEEP GOAL LIKE
PEPE

Punching, catching, kicking, saving. Liverpool's penalty-stopping, sweeper keeper is a master of them all

PLAY LIKE LIVERPOOL FC

Pepe on Punching

This is my own style.

I often prefer to punch the ball particularly as the Premier League is much more physical than Spain.

The referees are not the same here. In England it is typical to find a lot of physical games with a lot of crosses and direct play.

There are a lot of second balls that must be controlled. This is an important part of the game here.

In England you have some big, powerful centre-forwards so it becomes harder to get to the ball and catch it. You may not always get there comfortably so it can be easier and safer to punch it away.

I have always tried to be a forward-thinking goalkeeper

It is easer for the team to defend, if I can come out as far as possible.

We can hold a higher line and play further up the pitch. My role is to stay focused and play a little more advanced. I played this way for Villarreal and am comfortable with it.

I have the advantage of knowing how it works from Spain and the manager knew I played like this before I came to Liverpool.

At Barcelona and Villarreal I have always played in similar teams to here, teams that don't concede many goals and restrict the opposition to few chances.

We have that Spanish mentality here at Liverpool. I don't get a lot of work to do because we are so strong defensively.

I suppose a team like Real Madrid are an exception because they aren't always well-balanced defensively so the keeper will have much more to do but, certainly, the teams I have played for, the keeper has always had less work to do.

I think this is maybe the future for goalkeepers. I have always tried to be a forward-thinking, modern goalkeeper and believe that here at Liverpool I am getting some of the best training to help me achieve this.

KEEP GOAL LIKE PEPE

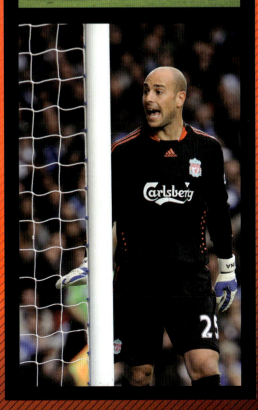

Stay on your toes

I always work on the idea that I will have to make at least three or four saves in a game.

That is my job in the team and it is important to stay focused at all times, to know when to stay or go out in between the lines.

The defensive unit tend to help you along during games but the main thing at a massive club like Liverpool is to ensure you make those crucial saves when they come along, no matter how few or many there may be.

Keeping a clean sheet

It is normal for people to look to the goalkeeper when the team is keeping so many clean sheets as we often do, simply because it is his job to stop the goals going in.

But as soon as you let one in you are open to criticism.

In my first season with Liverpool we went 11 games without conceding a goal. That was a great achievement but it was down to the defensive system as a whole.

Any credit for the success of the defence is down to the whole team rather than just me. It comes from the first attacker right back to me. It is the whole unit.

PLAY LIKE LIVERPOOL FC

SKILL TIP...

SAVING PENALTIES: With his heroics in the 2006 FA Cup final and 2007 Champions League penalty shoot-outs against West Ham and Chelsea, Pepe Reina has established himself as one of the greatest penalty-saving goalkeepers in world football.

How does he do it? He's not saying! Pepe has his own unique technique for saving penalties and doesn't want to give those taking spot-kicks an advantage by revealing what he does.

Most goalkeepers have different approaches to facing penalties - Bruce Grobbelaar and Jerzy Dudek famously put their opponents off by dancing on their line - but there are some general rules to follow, the first being 'always dive'.

There is more chance of saving the ball if you dive and even if it is struck down the middle you may be able to block it.

Most keepers decide which way to dive before the kick is taken. If you know your opponent usually aims for a particular corner then dive in that direction or, as a more general rule, right-footed players will aim to the goalkeeper's left and left-footed players to their right. Trust your instincts.

Diving before it is kicked makes it easy for your opponent to send you the wrong way so you should dive only when the ball is struck. Watching a player's body shape as he strikes the ball can also give you a clue as to where he is going to place it, but looking into his eyes can be deceptive as some players will glance towards one corner then hit it towards the other. If you do save the ball then it is crucial to get back to your feet as quickly as possible to try to save any rebound.

KEEP GOAL LIKE PEPE

SKILL TIP...

SETTING UP ATTACKS: A goalkeeper can be a valuable source of creating attacks for a team so it is important to work on your distribution.

As soon as you get hold of the ball you should be looking to distribute it quickly. Look for a teammate in space or a teammate sprinting forward and then try to find him with a long throw or kick. Throwing usually allows for greater accuracy.

However, if there isn't anyone available then don't simply boot the ball upfield aimlessly as you'll just hand possession back to your opponents. Always aim for a team-mate.

Practice your kicking and throwing regularly by aiming for a friend in different positions on the halfway line.

155

| PLAY LIKE LIVERPOOL FC

TRAINING TIP...

REFLEXES AND REACTIONS: Agility, quick reactions and reflexes are necessities for goalkeepers. These are improved by training.

One of the most common drills is to practice saving rapid fire shots that make you dive to your left and right for as long as you can.

Using several footballs lined up, get a mate to shoot low to your left then, as you get to your feet as quickly as possible, shoot low to your right and so on. This drill prepares you for match situations where you may need to make a second or third save after initially parrying the ball.

Another exercise involves getting a mate to stand a yard in front of you holding two balls, one in either hand, and throw them at you simultaneously. As he does so he must shout 'left' or 'right' and whichever he shouts is the one you must save.

You should also practice collecting the ball at different heights and in different weather conditions, particularly the wet.

Remember, a good goalkeeper always keeps on his toes so he is ready to react to anything and clutches the ball with 'soft hands,' arms extended and bends his elbows to absorb the pace on the ball.

Be vocal, be dominant, be confident and give defenders clear instructions. It's your box!

KEEP GOAL LIKE PEPE

MANAGE LIKE RAFA

MANAGE LIKE
RAFA

If you want to play for Liverpool then you've got to prove yourself to the manager. Rafa Benitez looks for certain qualities in every player

PLAY LIKE LIVERPOOL FC

RAFA SAYS...

The winning qualities we look for in a Liverpool player

The main thing is a winning mentality. They must have a winning mentality. A player must be hungry. After that you look for the quality of course and whether they are a good professional.

If you put those two factors together with the winning mentality, and the desire to come and play here and do well, these are the key factors that every Liverpool player must have.

Trying to sign players who will be able to cope with the demands of playing for LFC

When you know we could play around 60 games a season in so many different competitions, the quality and level of the player has to be right.

Sometimes when you sign a player you are expecting something from him but maybe he can not manage with the expectation here.

You have to analyse everything but try to sign players with ability and the right mentality to accept they may also be on the bench sometimes at a top club like Liverpool.

MANAGE LIKE RAFA

A winning mentality and the desire to come and play here and do well are the key factors that every Liverpool player must have and they have to accept they may also be on the bench sometimes

> You cannot win anything on your own. It has to be done with a good team behind you and working alongside you

We try to look for players who can represent the club in the right way on and off the pitch

We always look for good professionals and good people but we can't always guarantee these things nowadays. Society has changed and players are on big, big money. They are young people and you cannot control everything.

I'm not saying we have to look for the perfect role model every time but it helps if we can find good professionals. You can't control everything but these are the kind of people we want to represent Liverpool Football Club.

We have good technical staff and also the scouts who know what kind of players we are looking for. Part of their job is to ensure the players are good professionals and good people. Of course, you can't always guarantee this because people change, but we always use as much information as we can before we bring someone to the club.

As well as good players, you need to have the right people on your backroom staff

Clearly, you cannot win anything on your own. It has to be done with a good team behind you and working alongside you.

This is why it is vitally important to have the right people on our staff, so we can all work together towards the same goals.

MANAGE LIKE RAFA

Even if you have talent you need to work hard

The main thing is to keep the passion and the belief while continuing to work hard.

If you have the talent it is easier of course. But even then you still have to work at it. If you have the talent but don't work very, very hard, then you cannot be at a top club for long.

That is why even those players who have a lot of natural ability still have to keep working hard.

If you don't have that same level of talent it is more important to keep working hard. With hard work these players can still be footballers for a long time in the professional game.

Try to believe that you can play for a top side

This is also important. Together with the right mentality a player must have confidence in themselves.

Sometimes a player may be good enough but because they don't believe in themselves it prevents them from playing for a top side. It is important to have the quality and the skills but also the right mentality and confidence to do the things that will help you become successful in the game.

The right support from parents can really help

In Spain we talk about girls who may have potential as a singer but the singer can be lost with the wrong sort of intervention of the mother.

You might also apply this to football in that the player may be lost because of the father.

It is important to give your child good advice. Push, but not too hard while understanding the feelings of your son.

Support the son but also respect the coaches who are working with him. If a parent wants to be too involved they can actually be a bad influence on the nurturing and coaching process.

A parent has to respect, protect and push in the right way.

Training is the only way to really improve your game

Training is very, very important. It is the only way to improve. If you don't possess the natural ability that some top players have, training regularly is the only way to make it as a professional player.

If you are good enough, training is the only way to ensure you will keep your place in a top side and stay there for a long time. You can maybe play some games for a big club but if you want to stay and have a good career there you have to train well and be professional.

The key to reaching the top and staying there

My approach has always been similar. When I was a player I always liked to train. I could see a lot of very good players close to me but who weren't playing at the level they could have been simply because they didn't have the right mentality.

The experience I had as a player and then after as a coach at different clubs showed me that to train properly and to train hard is the only way to succeed, especially if you want to stay at a good level for a long time.

Some people maybe have the talent that will help them to play at the top for a maximum of two to three years, but they will not stay there if they don't train well and act as good professionals should.

MANAGE LIKE RAFA

My experience along the way

I started coaching in the youth team of Real Madrid and was at the club for about 10 years. I worked at all levels from U16s up to U19s, then with the reserve team and the first team. That was all good experience before I went into management elsewhere.

I went to Extremadura, Osasuna and Real Valladolid; all different clubs at different levels in different divisions. I gained some fantastic experience along the way from managing in the Spanish Primera Division to the Segunda Division with Osasuna, Extremadura and Tenerife - experiencing promotion with the latter two of these clubs.

It was all good experience and also taught me that I would have to work very hard to get to the position I am in now.

You have to have confidence in yourself, believe that you can do it and keep working.

What I think makes a good manager

You will never find somebody who is 100 percent perfect. We are all human beings and so will encounter problems and make mistakes.

I believe you have to be good at analysing the game. That is a big part of any team's success, especially during the season when things can change from week to week, game to game.

You also have to be clever and bring in the right people to work with you. We have talked about the backroom staff, and it is important to give these people confidence too.

You also have to be organised and have the right ambition. Then, of course, you have to try to sign the right players. At the end of the day it is all down to the players more so than it is the manager.

Then you must be honest and fair with people. You can't treat everyone in the same way because people are different.

You have to put all of these things together if you want to try and be successful.

> At the end of the day it is down to the players more than the manager

PLAY LIKE LIVERPOOL FC

THINK LIKE
A LIVERPOOL PLAYER

You might have the talent to play for Liverpool but have you got the right mentality? At Anfield, you don't just play football with your feet - you use your head

JAMIE SAYS…

If you want to become a Liverpool player, you have to start thinking like a Liverpool player. That means being professional and trying to improve yourself at every corner. The best way to start that is by eating properly as I mentioned at the start of this book. It won't necessarily make your passing, finishing or tackling any better, but it will make you fitter and allow you to maintain a consistency when other players and teams are tiring in a game. When you are tired, sometimes your consistency in basic skills drop slightly, but a decent level of fitness will prevent this.

THINK LIKE A LIVERPOOL FC PLAYER

You need to be professional and try to improve yourself at every corner

PLAY LIKE LIVERPOOL FC

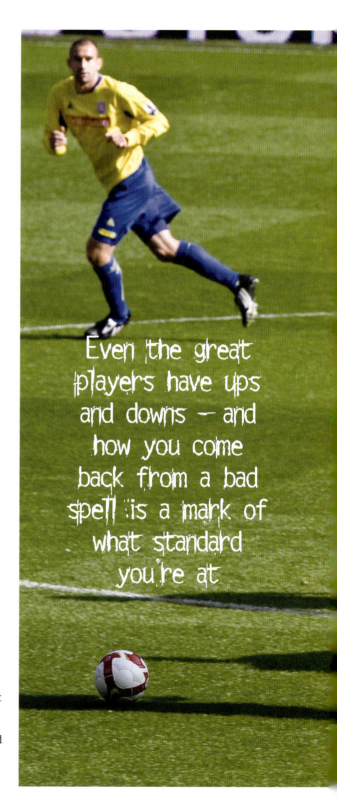

> Even the great players have ups and downs – and how you come back from a bad spell is a mark of what standard you're at

The best players never let their heads drop

The best Liverpool players are the ones with the right character. In that, I mean the players that won't let their heads drop when things are going against them. Every player has their ups and downs - even the great players - and how you come back from a bad spell is a mark of what standard you're at. I've grown up with a lot of talented footballers and witnessed some players at Liverpool arrive at the club for big fees and big reputations. But when they've been placed in front of 50,000 people who all want the team to win and things aren't going so well, these players just can't do it. It's not just a technical ability, but also a mental ability to never let things get to you.

THINK LIKE A LIVERPOOL FC PLAYER

PLAY LIKE LIVERPOOL FC

It's the Liverpool groove

Pass and move has always been the Liverpool groove and it is something every outfield player should get into the habit of doing. Never stand still and admire your pass. As soon as you lay the ball off you should be moving into space to give your teammate the option to play the ball back to you if necessary.

THINK LIKE A LIVERPOOL FC PLAYER

Be brave, be committed, be courageous

Bravery is a quality that earns a footballer the respect of his teammates, opponents and fans. Those who are prepared to do it for the shirt by putting their body on the line for their club are admired in football. Without courage and commitment, no team can be successful.

Give your all every time

Whether it's the Premier League or the park, the cup final or training, the minimum requirement in football is 100% effort. Give your all and try your best every time you play. If you don't put it in, you don't win.

PLAY LIKE LIVERPOOL FC

It's the Liverpool way

Modesty, a passion for the club and a desire to never give up is also important if you want to become a Liverpool player. These values are bred into players like me and Steven Gerrard who have come through the system and they have made us the players we are today. It's the Liverpool way.

PLAY LIKE LIVERPOOL FC

It's all about your attitude, your application and your talent

THINK LIKE A LIVERPOOL FC PLAYER

As one of our greatest players and managers, and now back at the club, Kenny Dalglish knows a thing or two about what it takes

KENNY SAYS...

Liverpool Football Club's not an ordinary place to play football.

You need to have something about you to make it to Liverpool, and then even more to make it at Liverpool. Arriving at the club's not the end of the journey. You've not made it when you get there.

The hard work's only just starting.

When you start out playing football, winning is not the most important thing. Enjoying the sport, loving having a ball at your feet and developing your skill levels are the most important thing.

Of course if you're winning games while you learn it's always a nice feeling but too much emphasis on winning trophies and beating teams doesn't always mean that you're developing correctly.

Success, real success, comes later.

If you go out onto the pitch with a win at all costs mentality then that's wrong. That's not to say that losing is ever something you should be altogether happy with.

You should be going out there to give everything you have inside yourself. You should be doing all that you can to help your teammates, to make something happen.

The best players know that it's a team game and that hard work, dedication and effort and the right mentality are more important than the final score at a young age.

Liverpool have done really, really well in the FA Youth Cup in the last couple of years and that's been great for the morale of everyone at the Academy.

But at the end of the day, for those boys, that's the beginning of their journey. Their real challenge is not to win that competition, it's to make it to the first-team at Liverpool.

Ultimately, winning those trophies won't decide whether you make the grade or not. It will be your attitude, your application and your talent.

You can win all the trophies in the world, but if you don't have those three it's going to be tough.

PLAY LIKE LIVERPOOL FC

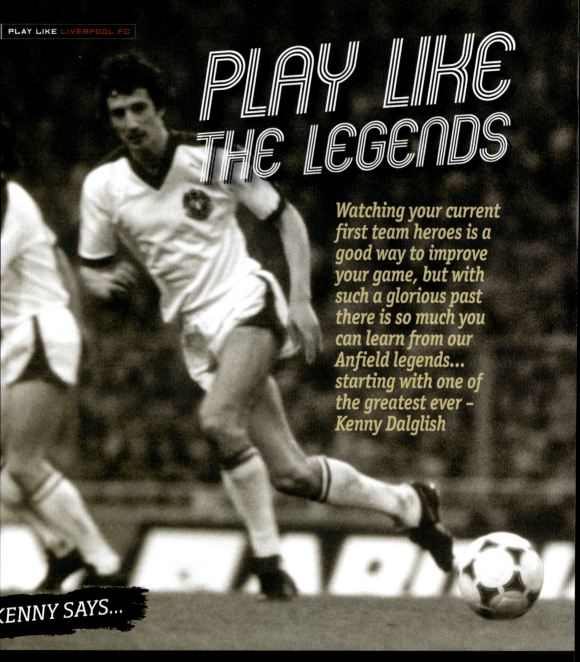

PLAY LIKE THE LEGENDS

Watching your current first team heroes is a good way to improve your game, but with such a glorious past there is so much you can learn from our Anfield legends... starting with one of the greatest ever – Kenny Dalglish

KENNY SAYS...

Find space for yourself

The most important thing you can do in the final third of the football pitch is to find space for yourself.

That doesn't matter whether you're playing in the World Cup final, the Premier League or down the park with your mates. You can't play football without space.

The easiest thing in the world to do is to be attracted to the ball, like a magnet.

But the trick is to let the ball, and your team-mates find you where you want to be.

You might not always get the ball where and when you want it. It doesn't happen like that even for Fernando Torres or Steven Gerrard every time.

But if you keep taking up the right positions inside the box and keep finding space then sooner rather than later the ball's going to get to you and you're going to get your chance in front of goal.

PLAY LIKE THE LEGENDS

Protect the ball

You have to protect the ball like it's the most precious thing in the world. If you don't have possession then you can't hope to score goals and if you keep giving it back to the opposition then you're making life tough for your team.

The way you do that is on an individual basis. When you take the ball into your feet, and there's an opponent close, use your body as a shield. If you're a forward and your back is to the man then stick your bum out, and it makes it almost impossible for him to come around you and take it off you before you can use it.

If your teammate has the ball and he's protecting it then it's your responsibility to find space and make yourself available for a pass.

One player moving into space for a pass isn't enough, you need two or three options every time you're on the ball.

PLAY LIKE LIVERPOOL FC

Defend from the front like Ian Rush

Ian Rush isn't just Liverpool's greatest ever goalscorer - he was also the Reds' first line of defence.

Defenders never got a moment's rest when Rush was about. He would chase them down, put them under pressure, make them nervous, force them to panic.

It stopped Liverpool's opponents playing from the back. Instead of having time and space to build attacks, defenders would be rushed - quite literally.

By pressurising them into mistakes and forcing them to hurry clearances, Rush would play a vital part in Liverpool winning back possession.

It was a particularly successful ploy at Anfield where teams would find themselves hemmed into their own half and, more often than not, under a barrage of Liverpool pressure, they would crack.

And the man who benefited most from Liverpool having so much of the ball was star striker... Ian Rush. With a record 346 goals for Liverpool, he's the perfect example of what can be achieved if you put in the hard graft.

PLAY LIKE THE LEGENDS

Shoot like Robbie Fowler

There is an art to goalscoring.
   Much of it is down to natural ability but technique also plays a major part. Take Robbie Fowler, for example.
   'God' was the most natural born goalscorer many Liverpool fans had ever seen but a lot of his clinical finishing was down to technique, particularly his ability to strike a ball first-time with little backlift. Fowler would hit shots quickly, with his head and knee over the ball but without lifting the foot he had shot with (usually his left) too high off the ground, or leaning back too much. By doing that, and striking the ball in the centre with his toes facing downwards and his heel facing up, Fowler was able to shoot with power and accuracy.

PLAY LIKE LIVERPOOL FC

DRIBBLE
LIKE THE LEGENDS

Peter Thompson

Flying '60s winger Thompson was a master at tormenting defenders with his swaying and twisting runs but he was also a right-footed winger who played on the left. His ability to dance past a man despite being on his unfavoured side showed how using both feet to dribble can give a winger the versatility to earn himself a place in the team.

Steve Heighway

Beating a man is only one part of the winger's job - using the ball effectively when you have done so is just as crucial. Steve Heighway could deceive a full-back using either foot by cutting inside, or hugging the touchline as he dashed down the outside at pace, but he could also cross the ball accurately with both feet. He was especially good at taking the ball to the byline before cutting it back to a teammate or drawing the keeper by faking a cross and then slotting the ball past him at his near post. Heighway's pin-point crossing and creativity was vital to Liverpool's success in the 1970s.

PLAY LIKE THE LEGENDS

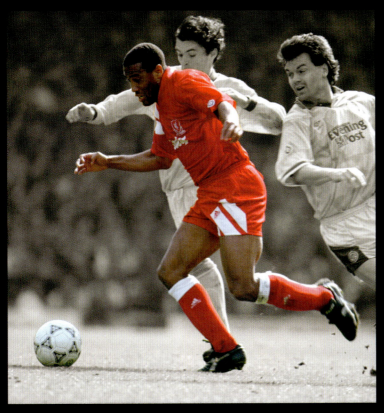

John Barnes

John Barnes didn't just dribble - he glided over the Anfield turf with the ball at his feet, twisting and turning defenders as he did so. He did so because of his balance. Barnes had a sublime first touch and an electric burst of pace but controlling the ball when running at high speed is no easy task. Barnes could do so because he used his arms to balance his body when running. He would feint to go one way by shifting his weight onto one side of his body but then push the ball to the other side. As defenders tried to readjust, his balance, strength and pace took him past them. It was exciting to watch and hugely effective.

Steve McManaman

One of the most crucial aspects of dribbling is close control and McManaman ran with the ball like it was tied to his boot with string. Macca's ability to beat a full-back was down to timing. His close control allowed him to 'show' the ball to a defender but as his opponent tried to win it he would skillfully snatch it away and jink past them in a split second. McManaman proved that you don't necessarily need blistering pace to be a top-class winger if you've got close control and immaculate timing.

PLAY LIKE LIVERPOOL FC

POWER & FINESSE

BOSS MIDFIELD LIKE THE LEGENDS

Graeme Souness

If you want to dominate the centre of midfield then you've got to make your presence felt. Graeme Souness did through aggression, power, and ferocious tackling. His drive and determination made him desperate to win every ball and his guts and bravery meant he never shirked a tackle. Players who put their bodies on the line earn respect from opponents. Souness had them living in fear.

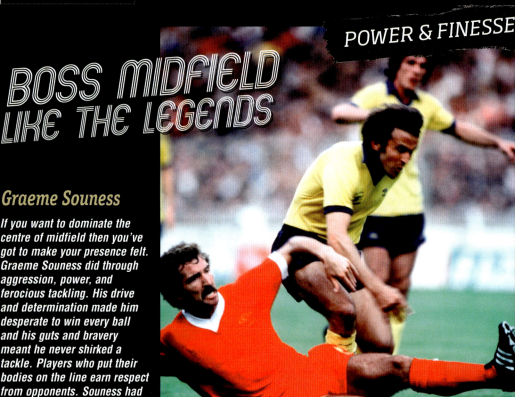

Steve McMahon

McMahon combined power with finesse. His win-at-all-costs attitude ensured that he worked hard when Liverpool had the ball and even harder when they didn't. The abrasive Scouser was an authority in midfield and was also noted for striking the ball with power. Anyone can smash a ball with force but doing so accurately takes practice. McMahon was adept at scoring spectacular goals from long-range. He was able to strike shots hard and low by getting his chest over the ball, or smash rising piledrivers with incredible accuracy. When such shots are hit on target, few goalies can keep them out.

PLAY LIKE THE LEGENDS

BOX-TO-BOX

Terry McDermott

Off-the-ball movement is an essential ingredient for midfielders and few were better at running from box-to-box than McDermott. His stamina levels and energy allowed him to do the hard yards and he was outstanding at ghosting into the penalty area from deep-lying positions to score goals. None are more famous than the flowing end-to-end move he started in one penalty box and finished in the other during the 7-0 win over Spurs in 1978. Many believe it is Anfield's greatest ever goal.

Ronnie Whelan

Football is a team game and every great side needs unselfish players. Whelan was one of them. His neat passing and running off the ball opened up space both for himself and teammates. One minute he'd be tackling outside his own box, the next he'd be curling home a beauty at the other end. Every team needs a Ronnie Whelan.

Jan Molby

Jan Molby arrived at Anfield looking hefty, sluggish and lacking the pace to play in English football. He left Liverpool with a reputation as the finest passer the club has ever seen. His trick? Creating time for himself on the ball. Molby let the ball do the work. His passing accuracy was of such a high standard that his first touch was often a pass. Rather than control a ball played in his direction he would simply lay it off again - and do so accurately. Molby would picture in his mind where his pass was going before he had received the ball, ensuring he was a step ahead of his opponents. Even when he took a touch, Molby would cushion the ball with his instep in the direction of where he was planning to pass it. Thinking what you are going to do with the ball before you receive it can give you a crucial advantage. The big Dane's first yard of pace was in his head and when Molby got into his passing rhythm, few teams were able to get near him or Liverpool.

TIME ON THE BALL

VERSATILITY & SWITCHING PLAY

PLAY LIKE THE LEGENDS

Ray Kennedy

Every footballer has a favourite position to play in but not many can perform to the best of their ability in different roles. Ray Kenney could. He was an established centre-forward when signed from Arsenal but Bob Paisley converted Ray into a left-sided midfielder. It was a masterstroke. Kennedy gave the Liverpool team balance with his ability to switch the ball from left to right through sweeping cross-field passes, often the key to breaking down stubborn defences. Kennedy also showed the value of a wide midfielder making late runs into the box when the ball is out on the other flank. He scored 72 goals for Liverpool, many of them coming when he arrived late at the far post to convert crosses. But it was Kennedy's versatility that made him such a valuable player for the Reds as he would sometimes play in a deeper midfield role, particularly in away European ties, before pushing forward late on to grab a valuable goal. Playing in different positions is something every young footballer should do. It helps to improve all-round skills and gives a manager options. You only have to look at Ray's medal collection to see where being versatile can lead.

DEFEND LIKE THE LEGENDS

Alan Hansen

Cool, calm and collected, Alan Hansen was an unflappable presence at the heart of the Liverpool defence. What he lacked in pace he made up in anticipation with his ability to read the game putting him one step ahead of the striker he was marking. He was also the finest ball-playing centre-half in the club's history. Hansen was sublime at bringing the ball out from the back to start Liverpool attacks. He'd glide over the ground like a hovercraft on the Everglades before playing slide-rule passes, often bypassing the midfield, for strikers to latch on to. It gave Liverpool an added attacking dimension, allowing the midfield to play further forward and hem teams in. Centre-backs receive a lot of the ball and the ability to use it well is a must in the modern day game.

PLAY LIKE THE LEGENDS

Tommy Smith and Gerry Byrne

Bravery and commitment are vital qualities that a defender must have. Tommy Smith and Gerry Byrne epitomised that. Smith was Liverpool's hard man in the '60s. Even if it was 30-70 against him winning the ball he wouldn't think twice about putting his foot in. Byrne took bravery to new heights when he played 117 minutes of the 1965 FA Cup final with a broken collar-bone and even set up Liverpool's opening goal. Both men were hard. Both were brave. Both were committed. Those qualities remain a necessity today for any defender. Give anything less than 100% and opponents will give you the runaround.

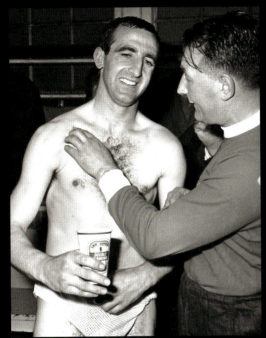

SAMI SAYS...

Heading it like Hyypia

People sometimes believe that to be good in the air you have to be tall, but that is not always the case.

Height is one factor, but it is not always the crucial factor when trying to head the ball.

Certainly, in my position I have benefited from being over six feet, that height has worked for me. But it is not essential to be a giant to play central defence well.

More important than how tall you are is your timing. If you get your leap correct and meet the ball before it starts to drop then you have a much better chance of making a good header.

Look at Jamie Carragher whom I partnered in defence for many years at Liverpool. Carra is not a massive guy, in terms of his height, but he has great aerial timing and a powerful jump so he is not beaten too often in the air.

There are things that you can practice without too much difficulty. All you need is a ball and some open space and you can practice for hours on end.

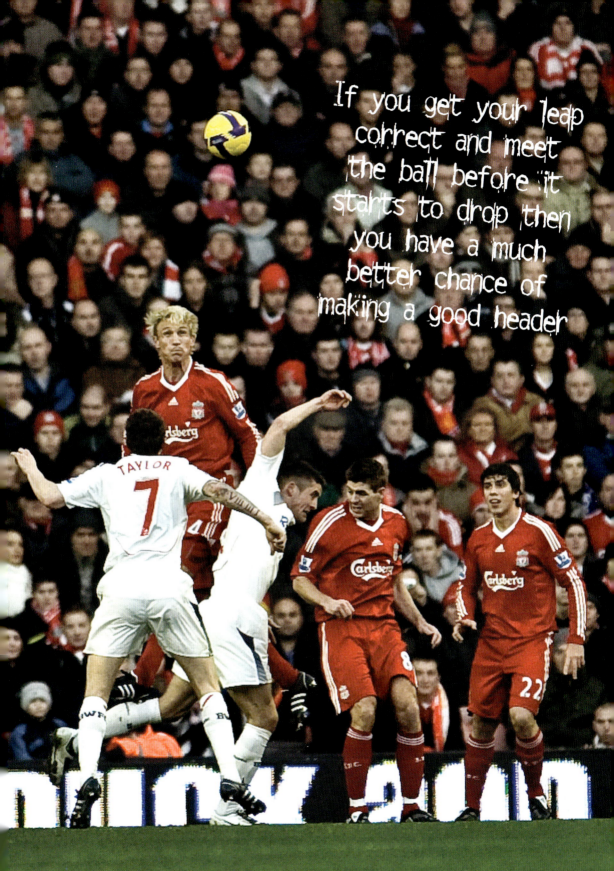

If you get your leap correct and meet the ball before it starts to drop then you have a much better chance of making a good header

PLAY LIKE LIVERPOOL FC

You don't need to be the tallest player

Heading is like every other aspect of football. If you work hard on it, and practice all the time, then you will get better and better in the air.

It's an important part of the game no matter what position you play in the outfield.

Torres is the perfect example of what I am saying. He is not the tallest player in the world but he is brilliant in the air.

That's simply because he can read the game very well, he has excellent anticipation, and his timing is always right. He is able to get into the air a split second before his opponent and that makes the difference in his position between getting a chance to score or not.

It is the same for defenders. The more quickly you can react to the situation and get into the air, the better.

PLAY LIKE THE LEGENDS

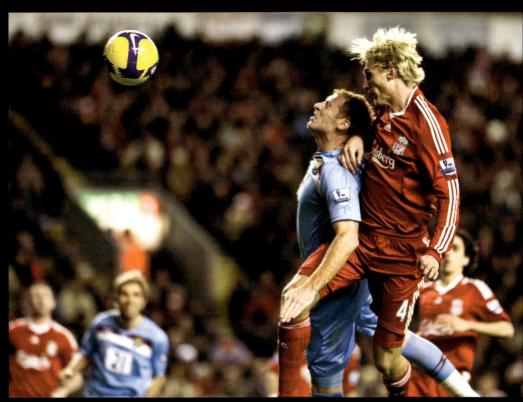

Bill Shankly

Tactical acumen, good man-management and the ability to lead are crucial qualities for any football manager to have.

Being able to motivate your players to perform is also absolutely vital and none were better than Bill Shankly at getting the most out of his men.

Shankly used psychology to make his players believe in themselves, to get them fit and as a weapon against opponents.

It was Shanks who changed Liverpool's kit to all-red as he felt it made the players look bigger and it was Shanks who harnessed the power of the Kop by using their amazing support to inspire his team.

He even put up the famous 'This Is Anfield' sign to "remind our lads who they're playing for, and to remind the opposition who they're playing against."

And it was Shankly who made his players believe they were invincible through his well-chosen words and motivational techniques.

In pre-season training he would start by holding practice matches on a full-sized pitch at Melwood but as the players got fitter the size of the pitch would reduce until eventually they were playing five-a-side in the penalty area.

Playing in such a confined space made the players improve their touch, passing and movement as there was no space to dwell on the

MANAGE LIKE THE LEGENDS

ball. Psychologically, they then found it easier to play on a full-size pitch again when the season started.

In the dressing room he would rubbish opponents, however good they were, before a game to convince his team they were guaranteed a win but then praise the opponents after Liverpool had won, telling his players they had just defeated a great team to boost their confidence.

At times he would be critical of his players in private but Shankly would always sing their praises in public.

On one occasion he told family members that goalkeeper Tommy Lawrence should have "been shot" for making a mistake yet moments later he told a journalist who phoned him that Lawrence was the "best goalkeeper in the world."

Shankly appreciated the value of confidence and positive thinking in football. Rather than undermine his players' confidence levels he would leave them feeling on top of the world.

Most of all, he made everyone connected with Liverpool Football Club - from the players and staff he assembled in the Anfield bootroom to the fans on the Kop - believe they were all part of the same team with a collective goal.

That togetherness and positive attitude were the cornerstones of Bill Shankly's Anfield revolution and the making of England's most successful football club.

Bob Paisley

Actions speak louder than words and that was the ethos of Bob Paisley's management style.

He never shouted or screamed at his players. He never went ballistic at a defeat or over-the-top at a victory.

Instead, he went about the job quietly, decisively and with authority, letting the team he sent out on to the pitch do the talking for him.

Paisley wasn't a charismatic, flamboyant individual like Bill Shankly. He was a softly-spoken man of few words but that was one of his strengths.

When Paisley spoke, the players listened. They knew that he only spoke when a point needed making.

Rather than fill their heads with all kinds of information, he kept things simple and his players listened more intently as a result.

But if they didn't listen to his instructions or perform to the levels expected, he would take action. Paisley thought nothing of dropping or even selling a player, no matter what he had achieved for Liverpool in the past.

Anyone who wasn't up to scratch was shipped out and that gave Paisley the respect, authority and fear factor a manager needs to have over his players.

Paisley also had a keen eye for spotting players in lower leagues and turning them into league title and European Cup winning stars.

Phil Neal was plucked from Northampton Town and became the most decorated Liverpool player of all time, Ian Rush was brought in from Chester City and turned into the Reds' greatest goalscorer of them all, Partick Thistle's Alan Hansen was developed into the classiest centre-half the club has ever had.

He would use the collective strength of the bootroom to coach players, with the likes of Joe Fagan, Ronnie Moran and Roy Evans all playing their parts, but utilise his own man-management skills to get the maximum out of his players.

Rush wanted to leave Liverpool when he wasn't being selected but after Paisley challenged him to be more selfish in front of goal he responded in sensational style, setting new goalscoring records.

The striker always had the talent, he just needed a manager to unlock it - although having Kenny Dalglish to play alongside certainly helped too!

Bob also had a knack of moving players to different positions to fit into his preferred 4-4-2 formation, which featured attack-minded but industrious wide midfielders rather than out-and-out wingers.

Ray Kennedy was signed as a striker but was converted into a wide left midfielder where he earned legendary status.

In his nine years in charge at Anfield, Bob Paisley's Liverpool won six league titles, three European Cups, three League Cups and one UEFA Cup.

He remains the only manager to have won three European Cups and he did so in a five-season spell.

For Bob Paisley, those trophies speak louder than words.

MANAGE LIKE THE LEGENDS

PLAY LIKE LIVERPOOL FC

CELEBRATE LIKE
THE PLAYERS

You've put in the graft, you've given your all, you've perfected your technique and you've just scored a cracker. There's only one thing to do - CELEBRATE!

PLAY LIKE LIVERPOOL FC

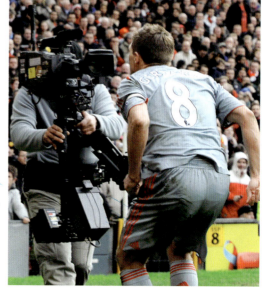

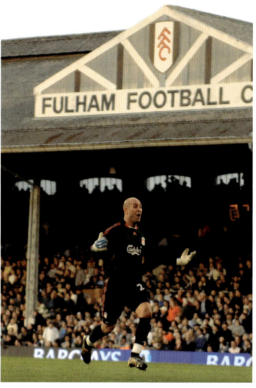

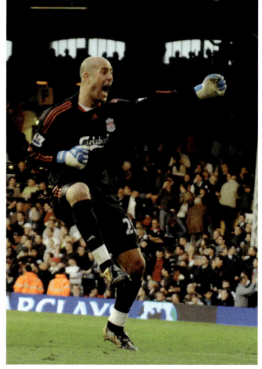

CELEBRATE LIKE LIVERPOOL FC

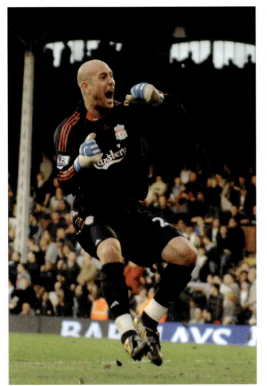
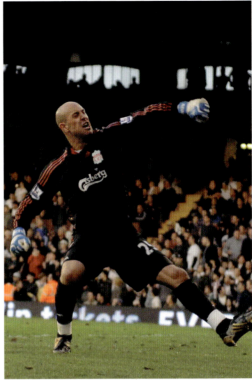
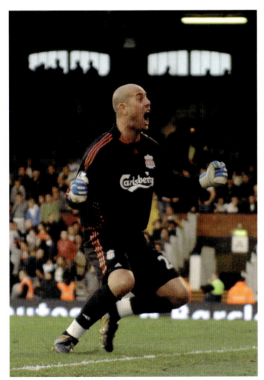

Football is a team game and you don't have to score a goal yourself to celebrate it. Enjoy the moment when your team puts the ball in the net as scoring goals is what football is all about. Pepe Reina showed the way to do it after a late Yossi Benayoun winner at Fulham

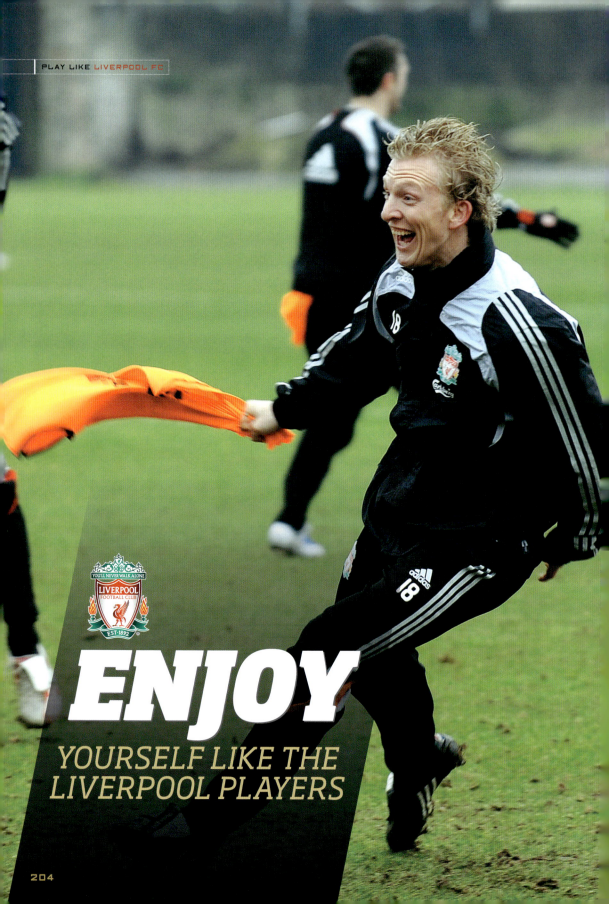

PLAY LIKE LIVERPOOL FC

ENJOY
YOURSELF LIKE THE LIVERPOOL PLAYERS

ENJOY YOURSELF

It takes a lot of hard work to reach the very top in football, but don't forget it should be something that you enjoy. It's a serious game when you are playing for Liverpool Football Club, but the players still find time for a bit of fun – it certainly helps with team morale

GOOD LUCK

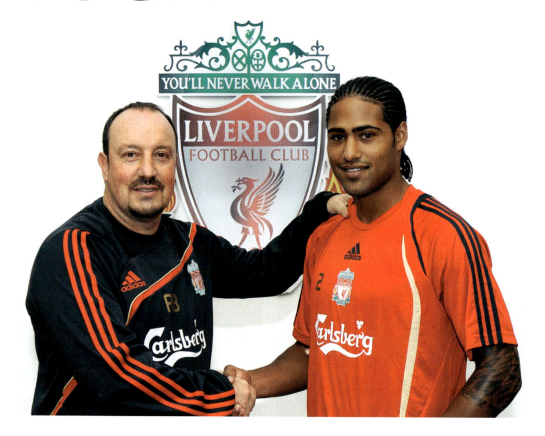

If you keep working hard, show quality, desire and have the right mentality then who knows maybe I will see you at Liverpool one day

I hope you have enjoyed reading Play Like Liverpool FC and that some of the skills and qualities we have been talking about can help you improve your game.

Now you must go and practice yourself. Even those players who have a lot of natural ability still have to keep working hard. If they don't then for me, they cannot be a Liverpool player.

If you don't have a high level of talent then it is more important to keep working hard.

With hard work these players can still be footballers for a long time in the professional game.

If you keep working hard, show quality, desire and have the right mentality then who knows – maybe I will see you at Liverpool one day.

Good luck.

Rafa Benitez

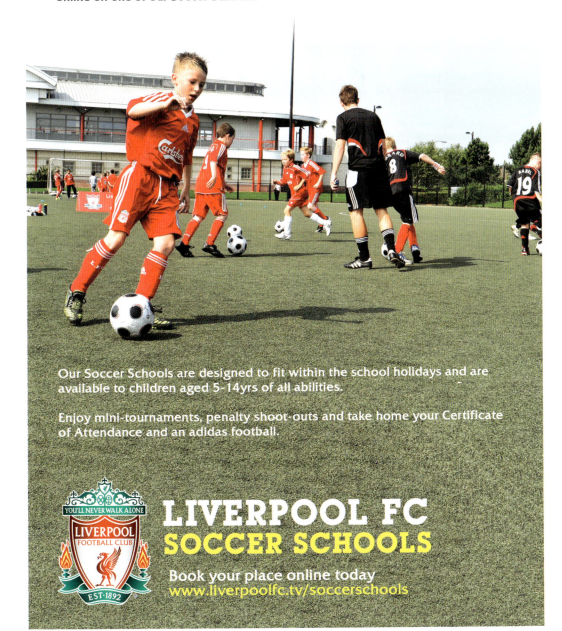

Other official LFC publications

LFC Magazine: Out every week. Red every day   LFC Posters: Packed with your Kop idols

 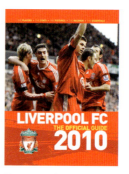

Players' stories behind the pictures   Your complete guide to 2010

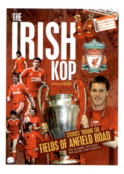 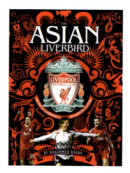

Story of Ireland's love affair with LFC   The rise of LFC in Eastern Culture

All of these titles, and more, are available to order by calling 0845 143 0001, or you can buy online at www.merseyshop.com